AND THEN SHE WOKE UP

HOW TO
RESTORY
YOUR LIFE

And Then She Woke Up: How to RESTORY Your Life

The book information is catalogued as follows;

Author Name(s): Katie Jones

Title: And Then She Woke Up: How to RESTORY Your Life

Description; First Edition

1st Edition, 2021

Book Design by Lynda Mangoro

ISBN (paperback): 978-1-913479-87-9

ISBN (ebook): 978-1-913479-88-6

Published by That Guy's House

www.ThatGuysHouse.com

AND THEN SHE WOKE UP

HOW TO RESTORY YOUR LIFE

7 STEPS TO YOUR HAPPILY EVER AFTER

KATIE JONES

CONTENTS

INTRODUCTION

Come with me … I want to take you to my favourite place. We're going into the woods!

Some people are scared of the woods, but not me. I think the woods are magical with the labyrinth of tree roots and branches, all entwining, all creating their own pathways. You cannot see where one tree starts and another one ends. Sometimes you cannot even see your way at all. The barks of the trees are covered with soft, velvety moss, and they are surrounded by crisp, fallen leaves, yet they each have their own story to tell. They stand tall, solid and rooted in the ground with their own markings, leaving a trace of their own unique tale.

In this enchanted place, the most incredible journey is waiting for you. If you choose to come with me, you will discover something truly magical. You will find a light that shines so brightly, it will lead you to true happiness. It will help you to see that no matter what has happened to you in your life, it is possible to transmute every single trauma into an opportunity to grow and evolve. Once you find it, you will be in possession of all the powers you need to overcome any challenges in your life. You will discover that nothing can defeat you. You will uncover the secrets to living a life filled with the most remarkable sense of freedom, contentment and fulfilment.

How do I know?

Because I have been here before. I've seen it with my very own eyes. I have completed this journey myself. It wasn't easy, but then again, how many of the most exciting adventures are? There were twists and turns. There were days when I felt lost and abandoned in the depths of the forest. Some days, I tripped and fell over the roots erupting from the earth. On dark nights, I trembled as shadows followed me. I fell into sharp branches, pulled out thorns and tended to my wounds. However, despite the setbacks, I continued putting one foot in front of the other, forging my own path until it led me all the way to the magnificent light. Once I uncovered the messages it held, I realised I was in possession of true happiness. And now I really want to show you.

I guess before you agree to come with me into the woods, you'll want to know who I am. Well, my name is Katie, and I think I am about eight years old, but I can't be 100% sure. You may wonder how I don't actually know how old I am. It's complicated. I have been hidden inside my adult-self for such a long time that I can't really remember how old I was when we got separated. But I think it was probably when I was around the age of eight.

I tried so many times to make myself heard and seen, but adult-me had been very good at pretending all these feelings didn't really exist. I'm sure the same is true for you, too. Inside you right now is an inner child who is probably trying to get your attention. Everyone has an inner child, and they know a lot more than most people realise. Your inner child knows how you can release yourself from your past hurts. Your inner child knows how to navigate through the forest, and how you can untangle yourself from the thick, thorny branches that are holding you back. Your inner child knows how you can reach the path that will lead you home to true happiness. Your inner child is the only one who knows the actual way. Nobody else can show you. Nobody else was there.

Having recently returned from the life-changing journey through the woods with my adult-self, I cannot wait to share it with you. Maybe you have experienced a major challenge in your life, and you are not sure how you will overcome it, or perhaps you are simply dissatisfied with your life as it is. Whatever your own situation, this book will lead you to creating your own 'Happily Ever After'.

I have called it the RESTORY journey as it takes you on a courageous adventure of deep transformation where you get to take control of the pen and decide how your story ends. It is just like Joseph Campbell's 'Hero's Journey', which has formed so many story structures of my favourite books and films. You'll recognise the much-used plot. At the beginning of the story, there is an everyday hero who is called to go on an epic adventure. Along the way, the hero learns valuable lessons, wins victories and then returns home transformed, in possession of the most magnificent reward. There are three key parts to the journey.

- **The departure**. The hero leaves the known world behind.

- **The initiation**. The hero learns to navigate the unknown world.

- **The return**. The hero returns to the known world with the reward.

Using this plot structure, I have created my very own RESTORY adventure for you to follow. There are seven steps, and they will lead you into the forest, partly because the forest is so magical and enchanting, but also because the forest represents the dark parts of our unconscious mind. These are the areas that remain unexplored, yet they are the parts that hold so many answers. The ancient, sacred trees of the forest contain so much wisdom, knowledge and powerful energy, and as soon as we shine a light on the shadows, we are able to illuminate these hidden parts of our being. By facing the shadows, we learn to trust, to follow our way home, free from limitations and filled with happiness.

The purpose of the RESTORY journey is to find the reward and to bring it back home. Guiding you towards the reward is a golden thread. I have placed this thread at various points through the seven stages, to help you navigate your way through the forest. You do not need to pull it or yank it, just gently follow it home. The thread holds key messages that will ultimately lead you to the reward. The reward has been hidden beneath layers of hurt and pain and once you uncover it and dust it off, it will shine with such spellbinding brilliance. Once you are in possession of it, you will want to share it with the world.

So, do you want to come with me?

THE RESTORY STEPS

These are the seven RESTORY steps that you will have to take if you wish to find the reward. They have to happen in this order, and you cannot skip any out. If you do, you will find yourself right back at the beginning. Trust me when I say it is much easier to follow the steps, in order, using the thread to guide you through the undergrowth.

Step 1 – Realise

You are living your ordinary life then out of the blue, you are presented with a wake-up call. Something knocks on the door of your conscious mind. The question is, are you willing to hear it?

The call to adventure can come in a number of different ways. One thing is certain, it will disrupt the comfort of your known world and present you with a challenge or quest that must be undertaken.

You have a choice here to answer the call or ignore it. The problem many people face is that this adventure may seem too overwhelming and the comfort of home in contrast is far more attractive than the perilous road ahead.

Step 2 - Explore

It's time to explore this realisation. You may go willingly, or you may be pushed, but either way, you will have to cross the threshold between the world you are familiar with and that which you are not.

This part of the journey will take you into the woods. They are dark, shadowy and the path is not always clear. There are strange noises, unfamiliar shapes and maybe tricksters waiting to trip you up. Are you brave enough to cross the threshold and step in? If so, you must accept that you will leave behind your known world and encounter parts of you that may have been buried for many years.

Step 3 - See the Shadows

As you journey deeper into the forest, you will come face to face with some unseen parts of yourself lurking in the shadows. This is where you are tested and confronted with some of the greatest challenges in your journey.

Even though this phase may feel deeply uncomfortable, you learn to face up and accept these shadows. By surrendering to the messages they hold, you start the death and rebirth process which is fundamental to your transformation.

Step 4 - Trust

Having surrendered to the shadows, you start to untangle yourself from the thorny branches. As you pull out the thorns, you notice something else deep within you. A sense of knowing, intuition, wisdom.

You no longer feel the crippling patterns of self-limiting beliefs, but instead a calmness washes over you. You start to feel safe enough to trust yourself.

Step 5 – Orientate

You hear the call to return back home to your known world. This is your time to return back with your newfound self-belief and inner contentment. You may still feel the familiar patterns trying to get hold of you and some days you may, in fact, tumble backwards. You have gone too far to accept defeat now. This is time to rise up and take ownership of your story.

You must now decide how you want your future to unfold. You must decide what values are important to you, what you really want, where you want to go.

Step 6 – Reclaim Your Power

As you begin the journey back home, you locate all the parts of yourself that had been lost over the years. Some may still be challenging, and you may still get caught up in the thorns. Perhaps their sharp spikes rip through you and reopen some of your healing wounds. Every time you snag yourself on these painful memories, you learn to heal with more kindness and more compassion. Soon there are no more thorns catching on your skin, and you are able to forge your own path with ease.

By embodying each and every aspect of yourself, you will feel whole and complete. You will rise stronger than ever before.

Step 7 – You Decide

You finally return home. You have the battle wounds, the scars and tiredness in your limbs to prove you have been on this epic adventure. But, despite this, you are lighter. You are no longer carrying around the weight of your secrets, your traumas and your past. You have faced the shadows of your unconscious mind and you have discovered the greatest gift: the ability to fully love and accept yourself.

Now that you are home, you are in possession of the reward which illuminates your path to living your life in true alignment. With this guiding light, you are now able to share your story with the world and inspire others to live their own 'Happily Ever After'.

WHO GETS TO BE THE HERO?

The heroes in my story books come in all shapes and sizes; from brave orphans, to feisty princesses, kind animals to cape wearing adventurers. The truth is anyone can be the hero in their own story. They just have to accept the call. I know how scary it can be to hear the call and worry whether or not to take it. I know first-hand, how terrifying it is to stand at the edge of the forest and gaze into the unknown, wondering what's lurking in the shadows, not recognising the strange, unfamiliar noises, not even sure if there is a path.

I know at times it seems easier to skip around the edges of the forest to get to the other side, but that never works. You cannot bypass the forest and hope to get to the same end destination. It doesn't work like that. You have to go inwards. You have to travel through the forest. It is the only way.

When you find yourself right in the midst of the forest, it is completely natural to feel afraid, but please try not to worry. This is all part of the process of healing. Every single person has the ability to venture through the woods. All we need is trust. We must trust that we are on the right path, even when we feel completely lost. Trust that we are following the breadcrumbs that will lead us back home.

To help us with this journey, I have created a map that will show the seven steps. Remember, you can't skip out a step: you have to go through each one. You may, at times, feel like you have been pulled back a step. That's ok – just pick yourself up and keep venturing forwards, one foot after the other.

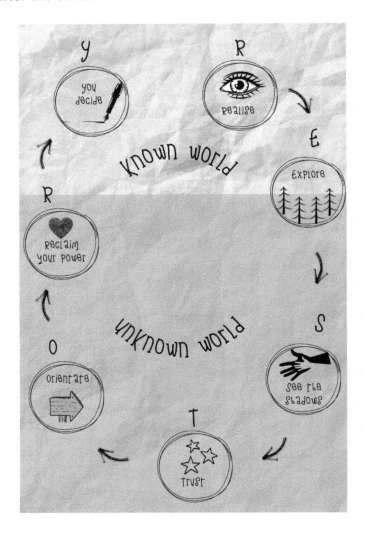

What is Your Story?

Have you ever thought about your story? What narrative about yourself do you carry around with you every single day? Where would you say your story sits on the shelves of a library? Is your life like that of an exciting fantasy novel, or is it more suited to the sad, tragic stories? Maybe yours is one of adventure or full of plot twists and surprises. Whatever section of the library your story fits into, the most important thing to remember is that it is yours. Nobody else's. Some might try and hold onto parts of your story and mistake it for their own. Equally, you may be holding onto to someone else's story, without realising it has nothing to do with you.

Your story is your story. The beginning has already happened. I suspect some of the middle has already been written, too. You may not like how it reads so far. They may be parts you wish you could rub out and start again. There may be characters that you feel ruin your storyline and divert your plot. That's ok. Whatever has happened up to this point has all happened for a reason. You cannot erase these parts. But, you do get to decide how you can learn and grow from them.

Spend a few moments considering your story. Are you ready to own it? All of it? Even the parts that make you angry? Even the chapters that have caused you pain? Even the characters that have led to grief and loss? I wonder if you were to describe your story now, what role have you given yourself? Are you a brave warrior who has overcome great challenges and emerged as a hero? Or are you a poor damsel in distress?

Think about all the different story lines in your life: work, family, friends, health, relationships. How are they going for you right now? How would you like them to be? If you choose to RESTORY your life, you can ensure you are the narrator: you get to decide how your life unfolds.

RESTORY-ING YOUR NARRATIVE

Do you find yourself following the same patterns over and over again? Many people find that they get stuck in a particular way of thinking, which keeps them stuck in a certain narrative. The wonderful thing about us human beings is that we have a brain which is like plasticine, meaning it is really flexible and we get to mould it. I love playing with plasticine as no matter how many times I make a mistake, I get to have another go and re-mould it until I get it right. It reminds me of the time when I learned to ride my bike. The first time I tried to pedal, balance and steer all at the same, it was really difficult. I wobbled lots and I kept falling off. But I didn't just leave the bike on the floor and decide cycling wasn't for me. I kept trying. My brain was working just like a physical muscle, and the more I used it, the stronger it got. The brain loves following a pattern, so the more times I practised riding my bike, and the neurons in my brain were activated in a particular way, the faster and easier it was for my brain to repeat the same pattern in the future.

This shows us that we can therefore mould our brains to follow a path of hope, optimism, empowerment and happiness and not continue to follow the well-trodden path of negative thought patterns.

Every minute of every day we have an opportunity to reframe our life experiences and change our neural pathways, but we have to want to do it. It is not going to happen by chance. By setting a clear intention, it is possible to RESTORY your life, minimise the wobbles and bring it back into balance.

Who is Future-You?

So, let's set the intention now. Who would you really like to be at the end of your journey? Imagine if there were no rules and absolutely nothing holding you back. How would you like your life to look? Imagine in the future someone picks up your story book, how would you like the blurb on the back cover to read? Be bold. What sort of character are you? How do you spend your days? What are your core values? You may have a really clear vision of what future-you looks like. If you can, this is fantastic. Keep hold of this image. Maybe write it down, draw it, document it somehow.

You may find it difficult to imagine who that future-you is featured on the back cover of your book. Sometimes, imagining a life which is different to this one can seem too much. Perhaps think about what things are holding you back right now. What would you like to let go of? What are some of the limiting beliefs you have about yourself? Maybe your future self can simply be you as you are today but without all that stuff weighing you down. Imagine how light you would feel if you didn't have to carry all that around with you every day. How would it feel to be fully in alignment with your values and to be following your true purpose in life?

Your Inner Child as Your Guide

RESTORY-ing your life may sound like a daunting task, but remember, you do not have to do it alone. Your inner child can help you with every step on this journey. Don't forget I am an inner child and I have travelled this path with my adult-self. The role of the inner child is essential on this journey. Remember, your inner child has been with you the whole time as you have been writing your own story. You probably assumed you left them long ago, the day you started to grow up, to find independence, to step into adulthood. You have probably placed them in the early chapters of your life and assigned them to the past. But they are very much part of your present. Inside of you right now is your inner child who has witnessed your entire story being written.

Chances are your inner child has tried numerous times to reconnect with you, to help steer you, but you have probably been too busy to acknowledge their existence. Don't feel guilty for doing this. Everyone does it. But I am here to show you that your inner child holds so many answers to help guide you on your path to becoming the best version of yourself, free from pain and suffering.

Your inner child resides in your unconscious mind, and you have probably been ignoring them, so that you can avoid the pain they hold. Irrespective of how nurturing your upbringing was, you will have experienced some pain and suffering at some point in your childhood, no matter how minor. You may not remember it, but this will have wounded your inner child. Your wounded child doesn't then just suddenly go away when you become an adult. You carry them within your unconscious mind and they often hide away feeling abandoned, rejected and unloved.

Your wounded inner child is often in the driving seat of your adult selves, influencing how you live your lives. Many of you will still be holding onto sadness, hurt and anger that resulted from external events in your childhood. Whether it was not being invited to a party or being called stupid in the classroom. Not being given any physical attention by your parents or shamed by family members. Feeling responsible for your parents' happiness or living with abuse.

So how do you recognise if you have a wounded inner child? We are usually crying out for attention, love, acceptance.

We crave it yet so often you find it really hard to love yourselves and accept praise. You may have low self-worth and lack confidence. You may look to others to fill the void or you may push people away. You may be people pleasers, be overly controlling, neglect your own needs, have difficulty resolving conflicts or indeed deliberately seek out conflict. Whatever the emotions your wounded child is feeling, it's highly likely that you are doing your best at ignoring them.

Every now and then, you may catch a glimpse of your inner child or feel them tugging on your heart strings, but then you shove down those emotions and carry on as if we were never there. We are always here. We never went away. We are simply waiting for you to find us again.

We are watching you live your life according to the old script, that outdated narrative. You have gathered together all the events of your life, assigned them meaning and, in many cases, they have created limitations. So many of you are not following your true life's purpose, and that is making you miserable. But, you have simply accepted it. It doesn't have to be that way. The RESTORY method will show you that you have the power to take hold of the pen and decide how the next chapters of your life will unfold. It isn't down to chance or luck. It is entirely down to you taking responsibility and deciding how you want to live your life. You honestly do get to write your very own 'Happily Ever After.'

Whilst you may not believe in fairy tales, and you may not even believe that magic exists, I am here to show you that no matter what has happened in your life, it is always possible to turn it round into something magical. Every single person has a path waiting to lead them back home to their true self. It is not suddenly going to appear in a puff of smoke. You cannot wait for Prince Charming to come and save you. You cannot expect a Fairy Godmother to wave her magic wand. This is your story and it needs you, the protagonist. So, who are you? The victim or the hero? It's up to you to decide who you want to be. Then you must take action. You cannot sit around waiting to be saved. Your destiny is in your own hands.

BUT...

As you read this, you may already have started to gather all the reasons why you don't have time to go on adventures right now. Too busy ... Too stressed ... Too tired ... Not enough hours in the day ... We all have the same 24 hours in a day. It's up to us how we prioritise them. If you want to get the most out of your life, then you need to take action and set off on the epic adventure waiting for you.

In order to RESTORY our lives, we need to shift the perspective, and rather than life happening TO us, we start to see through the lens of life happening FOR us. Imagine you have two different pairs of glasses. Through one pair of glasses, you are the victim in your life and everything bad is happening to you. Through the other pair of glasses, everything that happens in your life is viewed as an opportunity for you to grow and evolve. To come on the RESTORY journey, you need to wear the second pair of glasses.

One way to view this is to imagine you fall off a cliff edge and you are headed towards a crevasse, where you will certainly hit the rock and shatter into a million pieces. If you are wearing the first pair of glasses, you will think 'Why does this always happen to me?' and most likely, you will hit rock bottom and remain shattered. However, if you choose to wear the second pair of glasses, you will discover at the bottom of the crevasse there is a trampoline. As you land on the trampoline, the bounce back is so powerful it will propel you back up to the cliff edge and then way beyond. Beyond into a world that you never knew existed. This is how we learn to grow from our challenges.

Thankfully, without even realising she was doing it, adult-me had gone through her life largely wearing the second pair of glasses. That doesn't mean she avoided any challenges in her life and everything was rose-tinted. She had experienced some devastating tests and hit some major rock bottoms, but she didn't allow it to be the end of her. She always chose to bounce back and into a world that offered more joy and happiness.

Let me share her story with you.

Once Upon a Time

Once upon a time there was a little Welsh girl, called Katie, whose hair glistened in the sun like golden thread. She was a happy, impish child, who loved playing in the long grass, and was captivated by the magic of fairies and elves. Times had not been easy for her parents, and they sadly divorced when she was a baby. Their differences of opinion made it impossible for them to be civil to one another and as their bitterness grew, their lives became filled with anger and resentment. Her mother was a hard-working, single parent and had to focus on keeping the family fed and clothed. Her father was an artistic soul who wished for a life full of excitement and adventure.

Katie grew up with a deep desire to please other people. She had learned from a young age that she had to be a 'good girl'. She wanted to be liked by all, but this was proving rather challenging. Her brother was angry with life and used her as his punching bag. Her mother was too busy surviving. Her father was too distracted looking for adventure in the bottom of a beer can.

Katie was very good at being a good girl. To the outside world she was a happy, sociable child. She did well in school, was a prefect, a girl guide, loved art, dance and gymnastics. She tried her very best to please people, but it never filled the deep void inside of her.

This eventually got too much for Katie, and in her teenage years she started to take big risks in her life. She was now desperate to find love and happiness in her external world. She started experimenting with alcohol and drugs and the deeper she fell into this rabbit hole of self-destruction, the harder it was to get out. Her relationships with her own family were not improving, which sent her further into the darkness to find love.

Katie tried to find comfort in the beds of one-night stands, but that left her feeling full of self-loathing and self-hatred. She tried to find it in cigarette packets, but that left her feeling dirty and penniless. She tried to find it in dark, sticky bars in the early hours of the morning, but that left her feeling sick and empty. She tried to find it in white powders and pills, but that left her feeling full of shame and regret.

Then, one day, as if by magic she found herself transported to another life. If she believed in Fairy Godmothers, she would say she had been granted a magnificent wish to begin a new life in London. She not only found herself with a promising job but also on a blind date with a tall, dark, handsome recruitment consultant.

After months of courting, he whisked her away to his trendy flat in Notting Hill and opened her eyes to a whole new world, filled with love, laughter and adventures. Life certainly started to look up for once. Her handsome prince was able to see through her rough edges and gave her unconditional love and patience as she started this next chapter in her journey.

Sadly, just as life was beginning to improve, she experienced the gut-wrenching deep grief when her father died from alcohol abuse, aged 51. He had been consumed by the lure of a life of adventure which in fact had simply given him a bedsit filled with overdue bills, empty vodka bottles and piles of vomit. The following year, her stepfather died suddenly whilst on a walking holiday in France. Katie was in her mid-twenties and experiencing incredible pain that was splitting her heart in two.

Despite this sadness and loss, thankfully her own family started to grow. Her ever-loving husband and two beautiful children set up home in rural Oxfordshire. She had a warm and nurturing home, an incredible family of her own and a constant stream of love from her husband. She started to follow her curiosity into the spiritual world and trained as a yoga teacher, reiki healer and children's wellbeing teacher. She had created a wonderful life, abundant in so many ways.

Then one day, out of the blue when she was 41, Katie had a sudden realisation that she had been sexually abused as a child by a family member. The memory catapulted itself from the depths of her being and spilled out all over the floor. This horrifying realisation was her call to adventure.

The question was, was she strong enough to explore this further and enter the woods? This was the moment she made a monumental decision. She was not going to accept defeat. She was not prepared to be the victim in her story. She had already faced the challenges of her parents' divorce, her father's alcoholism, his subsequent death, followed by that of her stepfather. She had come this far. She was not going to give in now. This is where Katie chose to venture onto the hero's journey to find deep inner transformation. This was her chance to leave her known world and follow her path back to her true self. Katie took the courageous step to answer the call and start her epic adventure. This was the moment Katie decided to RESTORY her life...

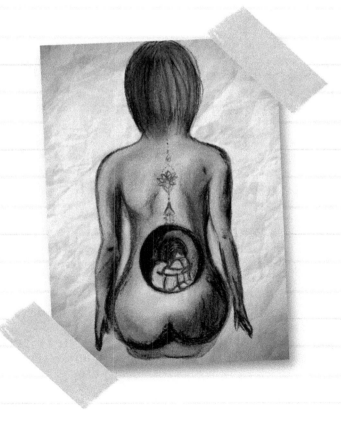

YOU ARE NOT ALONE

As you can see, adult-me had been pushed out of the comfort of her known world, and she found herself crossing the threshold into an unfamiliar world. However, she did not have to journey alone. I was with her the whole way.

No matter what trauma you may have faced, it is always possible to RESTORY your life and you do not have to do it alone. Take hold of your inner child's hand and allow them to lead you on your way. Just as I led adult-me on her own journey through the woods.

Part 1 of the RESTORY journey is written by me. I explain what happened to adult-me at each of the seven steps. I have chosen not to disclose who the family member was who abused me. This was a difficult decision as part of me wanted to shout and scream it from the rooftops, to let everyone know exactly what sort of man he was. But I have chosen to keep that information confidential, at least for now.

I also encouraged adult-me to draw pictures and write poems to express her innermost feelings. She found these bursts of creativity enabled her to release the intensity of the emotions and as soon as they were on the page, they made a little more space inside of her. She was so nervous to share her drawings and poems with anyone else. She was embarrassed that people would think they were no good. But as I told her over and over, they were an honest, raw, real, uncensored and brave expression of how she was feeling during these dark times. She had to share them. She had to be brave. I'm so glad she did as they have enabled me to be seen and heard. As you look at her drawings and read her poems, see if they stir something inside of you. See if you can feel your inner child willing you to be brave.

Right now, there are so many other brave, courageous women, rising, finding the courage to RESTORY their lives and share their tale. It is through the gathering together of these incredible storytellers and truthtellers that we get to change our narrative. We are not victims. We are heroes. Come join me as we discover the magic of the RESTORY journey.

Sisters

Sisters, I hear you, I feel you, I'm with you.

Let go of the shell that's held you so tight,
You don't need to bind yourself day and night.
Break free from the confines of what you ought to do,
Be who you are. Be true to you.
Sisters, allow the tears to fall,
Let them gather in a pool awaiting us all.
We feel the pain. We know the fear.
You are not alone. You are held near.
Listen to the whispers. They are all around.
Listen to the trees that root us to the ground.
Be held by the feminine embrace of each other,
Surrender your fears and truly discover.
You are a warrior. You have what it takes.
Pull out the thorns. Discard the stakes.
Feel the power rise through your veins,
Release the shackles, take hold of the reins.

Sisters, I hear you. Sisters, I feel you.

Gathering together entwined as one,
Sisters, Rise! There's work to be done.
Call on the earth, air, water and fire.
Let love flow through you with burning desire.
Know that the pain is a sign to behold,
That you are alive with a story to be told.

Peel back the layers. Allow the light to shine.
You are ready. This is your time.
Stand your ground with tenderness and grace,
Allow the love to radiate from your face.
Let's journey together, deep into the unknown,
Travelling through the woods, leading us home.
Sisters, it's time to unite with your power,
This is your life, this is your hour.

Sisters, I feel you.
Sisters, I hear you.
Sisters, I'm with you.

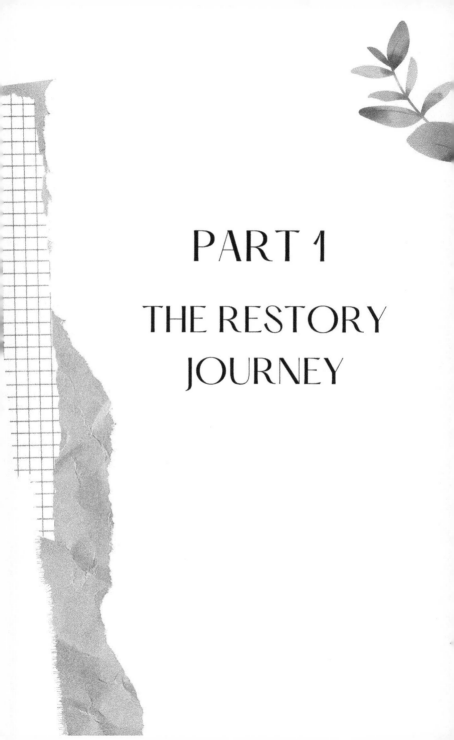

PART 1

THE RESTORY JOURNEY

STEP 1 – REALISE

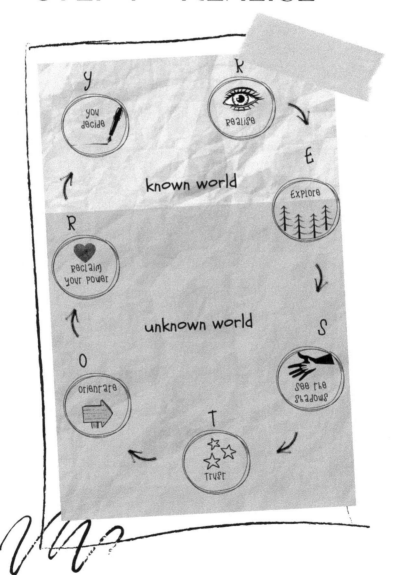

realise

There comes a time when the Universe grabs us by the ankles and shakes us upside-down in order to truly wake us up to the reality of our known world. If we are willing to answer the call, then we will be propelled forwards into great uncertainty. The other side of the uncertainty is tremendous transformation. The call to adventure requires an enormous leap of faith. You will never know how the adventure is going to unfold. The only certainty is that by journeying through the woods, you will emerge the other side completely transformed. Are you willing to wake yourself up and take the giant leap into the unknown? Are you ready to transform into your most authentic self?

Let's set the scene of how the RESTORY journey began. Imagine you have opened the pages of a much-loved fairy tale book and you have encountered the protagonist living a wholesome life. One where she was surrounded by love and warmth, and the smile on her face depicted a life filled with joy. The sun shone brightly, the birds sang sweetly, and everything seemed 'just right'. That would certainly be how you could describe my adult-self's life if you were an observer looking in. Adult-me was living in a beautiful village in rural Oxfordshire. She had been happily married for 15 years. Her two gorgeous children were 10 and 13 years old. Her spare time was spent walking with her two spaniels, practising yoga, reiki and meditation. Her wellbeing business supporting children's mental health was thriving. On the surface, life seemed to be just like it had come out of the pages of a storybook. But in fact, the protagonist in this story was in a deep sleep. Adult-me was sleepwalking her way through her life without realising she was about to face the most colossal wakeup call.

Underneath the façade of my adult-self's wholesome, ordinary life, there was a hidden darkness that was starting to creep its way into her being. Without her realising it, the nearby forest had been calling her to embark on a life-changing adventure. The rampant vines of the wild, untamed branches had started to burrow into her conscious mind. Their smothering tendrils latched onto her thoughts and attempted to wake her up from her deep sleep. She wasn't ready to wake up. She focussed on distraction techniques, for sub-consciously she knew if she kept herself busy, the tendrils would lose their potency and they would eventually lessen their grip. She was an expert at occupying herself. She would have numerous projects on the go. She'd volunteer for multiple jobs and go out of her way to help other people. She was an avid people-pleaser. Like many people, she had used the badge of 'busy' as an effective means of distraction. Being busy was her safety blanket. It helped her to stay asleep.

Hidden amongst the busy-ness, in the depths of the forest, was me, her inner child, trying to get her attention. I wanted her to know that the call to adventure was waiting for her. I tried to scream and shout that there was a path through the forest that would lead her back home to her true purpose. But she couldn't see me or hear me. I was locked away. Maybe at times she had an inkling I was there, when she felt a tug inside of her, urging her to venture towards a different future. She definitely knew there was more to life. She had read about it in books and heard about it on all the spiritual awakening courses she had attended, but she still didn't know how to find it. She'd often grapple and pull at random threads, hoping they would lead her to this far-away existence of happiness. She didn't realise that the path to her dreams already existed.

I was trying to tell her. I wanted her to know the truth. I was holding the end of the thread that would lead her home. I had been holding it the entire time. I wanted her to know that she did not need to pull, yank or go searching for it. It was already here. She just needed to gently follow it back home. Back to me, her inner child. That was where all the answers lay.

One way I tried to get her attention was to remind her of a time when she felt really happy and free. The most powerful memory was when she was about five years old. She loved being outside in nature, playing with the insects, wildflowers, grass and soil. She would make great kingdoms out of these natural wonders that Mother Earth had gifted her. Hours would go by and she would hardly notice. She was completely in flow. Lost in her imagination. I remember one particularly hot summer when there was a huge swarm of ladybirds. They were everywhere. It was as if they had all come to play at once. She had so much fun collecting them and storing them in her pockets. She would spend hours playing with them in the garden, transported to the magical worlds within her own mind. This little girl was free, creative, filled with wonder, excitement and spontaneity. I tried to remind adult-me that this little girl was still part of her. She still had that ability to feel free, connected to nature and lost in her imagination. But adult-me chose to push these memories aside and carry on with her ordinary life.

Adult-me was sleepwalking in a direction that lacked real depth and meaning. Every so often when I tugged the thread to remind her of her true calling, she would feel it deeply. It was like a yearning to go home, a longing to remember who she was and what she came here to do. Your inner child is most likely doing the same, especially if you are not following your true path. We are often trying to get your attention to remind you of where home is. Sometimes you listen, but mostly you shove the feeling down and stick it in the box of emotions you desperately don't want to feel. Some of you pour wine on top of the box to drown it out. Some of you bury it with unhealthy food to try and stifle its cries. Some of you ignore it by mindlessly scrolling through social media as a means of distraction. Some of you will numb it out through prescription medication. You all have your own coping mechanisms. I just know you will do anything to avoid opening the box.

Adult-me was aware that she had shoved something in her box, and she guessed it was something pretty big. She had been harbouring deep-rooted issues of low self-esteem. I would even go as far as saying she secretly hated herself, but she had become very skilled at pretending. Pretending she was fine. Pretending she was happy. Pretending she was satisfied. She was so good at pretending that she had even managed to convince herself that the fake smile was true. She would look at herself in the mirror and pretend that all was well. But in reality, she could never actually fully look herself in the eye. She desperately wanted her reflection to reassure her that she was worthy and loveable, but she was terrified that pure evil was all that shone back in her face.

Adult-me was deeply uncomfortable with who she was, yet she didn't know why. She found the concept of self-love utterly bewildering. How on earth could she love this version of herself? She always felt like she was such a bad person, rotten to the core. She felt like she had been concealing a putrid monster deep within her, as if it had been hidden in a vile dungeon, locked away so nobody knew of its filthy existence.

I knew the truth. I knew why she felt this way. I tried to tell her, but she wouldn't listen. She just kept shoving these emotions down, and the box was getting fuller. I used to hear the box creaking at night-time with the weight of all the emotions that had been shoved down, buried, repressed. You might think by shoving these feelings in the box that they will go away but I can tell you they never go away; they just get louder and louder until, one day, the box will burst open and all the messy contents will spill out onto the floor. They will make your body ache, your muscles throb, your joints scream. This is exactly what was happening to adult-me. She had such a painful jaw; it was as if it was working so hard to keep everything silenced. Her chronic migraines were debilitating, and it seemed her head was screaming in desperation. Then one day, it could hold on no more.

She had tried so hard to keep this part of her hidden. She had drowned it out with wine. She had quietened it with busy-ness. She had ignored the groans and painted a smile upon her face. However, something was beginning to rumble deep from within her. There was a surging pulsation that was starting to shake her foundations. The tremors were felt throughout her whole body. Her jaw pain was reaching excruciating levels. Her headaches were agonising. The hypocentre of the earthquake was the box. It had been filled with so many repressed memories and emotions that it could no longer hold on. Its vibrations were reverberating through every cell in her body and then one summer's afternoon the box burst its lid, and out spewed every putrid secret that had been shoved down there. With horror, adult-me watched as the ugly, heinous words fell from her lips. 'I think I was sexually abused when I was little.'

The filthy, shameful presence of these words abruptly jolted her out of her known world. She did not want these words to fall from her lips. She had no idea where they came from. Yet their presence could never be retracted. She desperately did not want to believe this was true. This disgusting, repulsive plot twist was oozing out of her mouth like the most noxious, pus-filled horror and she could not stop it. It had a life force of its own. This was her call to adventure. She was being forced to wake up.

The Box

A nagging feeling,
in the pit of my gut.
I locked it away,
Closed it shut.
It's gnawing away,
at my sense of self.
Affecting my sleep,
my mood, my health.
I've tried to ignore it,
keep it at bay.
But it won't disappear,
it won't go away.
It stays with me,
both day and night.
Taunting me,
to brave the fight.
But I haven't got time,
there's too much in my life.
How could I possibly
deal with more strife?
Surely, it's better
to just push it back down.
Paint a smile on my face
and mask my frown?
Shove the emotions,
too painful to feel.

Into that box,
devised to conceal.
This isn't the first time,
it's come looking for me.
Yet this time I know,
I can no longer flee.
But what is down there?
I'm scared and afraid!
What will it show me?
What mess have I made?
The walls are now shaking,
threatening to crumble.
I lose my grip,
I lurch, and I stumble.
There is no choice,
but to venture down there.
And face this monster,
in its putrid lair.
The lid of the box,
bursts open wide.
Releasing the rancidity,
held deep inside.
My worlds collide,
fear and horror merge.
The vile secrets transpire,
as I begin to purge.

Expelling traces of shame,
as the reality hits home.
I feel so lost,
So scared, and alone.
Banishing this monster,
from the depths of my soul.
It leaves sheer terror,
And a gaping hole.

This was the moment adult-me was suddenly forced to wake up. One minute she was asleep, living her ordinary life. Then BAM! This secret exploded out of her. She had been abused as a child by a family member. It burst out of her like projectile vomit, spewing out with a power and life force of its own. She could no longer contain it. It was time for it to be expelled from her.

Adult-me had no idea that she had been living her life in such an amnesic sleep. It was as if she had been cursed and sentenced to living a life completely unaware of the secrets hidden deep inside of her. For so many years, she was totally unable to see or hear the truth. The curse enabled her to exist but not to fully live. She was sleepwalking through life in a bubble of oblivion that had been protecting her from the truth that lay before her.

I knew all along. I had tried to tell her, but she couldn't or wouldn't hear me. I was still locked away and I desperately wanted her to find me. All those years ago, when the abuse happened, I remember feeling really sad. I was also really scared as this was the moment that I got separated and lost. To the outside world, everything was carrying on just the same. My mother was still preoccupied with the challenges of being a single parent. My father and step-mum had just started their own family. I simply slipped unnoticed into a fake version of myself. That other version of me had learned to carry out the role of a good girl, to smile when required, to stifle emotions, to keep out of the way, to behave when asked, to get good grades at school. That version did as she was told and painted a smile upon her face and learned to be 'just fine'. She became so good at pretending, she even convinced herself. I, however, was completely lost and abandoned, locked away in a desolate cage, with this dark, heavy secret looming over me.

I watched from the darkness as this other part of me played out a role. It was like she was pretending to be

Katie, but she wasn't the real Katie. In protecting herself from the abuse that she experienced, she was further detaching from her truth. She was hiding away from the reality of her world. She was actually really good at it.

Over the years, I desperately tried to get her attention and tell her the truth. I would repeatedly knock on the door of her conscious mind and try to remind her of what was going on. I knew exactly what had happened, but I was also aware that her brain had protected her from the shocking truth. It had shut down the memory part so that she couldn't remember the horrific details.

This explains why when adult-me tried to remember our childhood, there was nothing there, just a big, black empty hole. Especially around the ages of seven to eleven years. It is as if all the memories were sucked out and she was left with a gaping chasm of nothingness. No memories remained of junior school. No memories remained of her childhood bedroom. No memories remained of her friends and her toys. There was just darkness. An emptiness that made her feel uncomfortable, but she didn't understand why. This is where I was hiding. This is why I cannot really be sure how old I am. I was lost somewhere in these years of confusion, disgust and shame.

There were a few upsetting memories that would circulate around my adult-self's head that really should have raised alarm bells, yet she diminished their significance and laughed them off. I remember these memories so vividly. One was when she used to regularly hit herself in the face with an old wooden recorder. She would stand in the dark, cold front room of our terraced house and repeatedly hit herself in the face. I can still recall the crack now as my cheekbone made contact with the wood and I can still feel the deep sense of relief as the physical pain washed over me.

Another is when she used to hide food under her bed until it started to rot. She was told she lived like a pig, but the truth was, it made her feel safe to be encircled by rotting substances. Watching the decay eating away at the remnants made her feel better. It was like she belonged.

She also had recurring nightmares of being trapped in a windowless room with no means of escape. For years, she was frequently tormented by the recurrence of an intimidating male presence that was overbearing and threatening, yet there was no way out. She had no option but to allow it to consume her. Night after night, the same nightmare would hijack her dreams, suffocating her with fear.

Whenever these memories would surface, along with the memories of the frequent urination in a house plant pot, and the discovery of a vibrator and knowing where to put it, my adult self would laugh them off and disregarded them as being an odd child. They hadn't yet woven their way into the narrative of her story. They were random, unrelated thoughts floating through space. In reality, this was probably the first time the realisation came knocking on the door, but adult-me wasn't ready. It happens quite often that we hear the whispers, but we doubt their existence. It's as if the branches of the ancient sacred trees from the deep dark forest have been tapping on the windowpane, enticing us to come explore the truth of our unconscious mind. As my adult-self was not fully awake when these memories surfaced, she continued to ignore their call.

This is not unusual when we first receive the call. We can ignore it, bury it, drown it out. The thought of answering the call can appear too daunting, so we do whatever we can to prevent it from opening us up to the truth. Adult-me found spending time alone in her own head a terrifying prospect, so she would fill every moment of every day to avoid the stillness, to fill the pauses, to prevent the truth from surfacing. If she was alone in the car, she would call someone. If she was going on a walk, she would listen to a podcast. If she had time to herself, she would endlessly scroll through social media.

On bad days, she would drown it out with alcohol. Having an alcoholic father, she had a rather confusing relationship with the stuff. She obviously knew how damaging it could be. She had witnessed her father unravel from being a charismatic, loving, artistic, gregarious man into an incoherent, aggressive, pitiful, vomit-stained mess. When he died at the age of 51, you would have thought that would have put an end to her reliance on alcohol to numb out pain. At times it did. She fluctuated from being tee-total for months on end to using it as a means of silencing the inner torment.

I do often sit and wonder what it was our dad was so desperately running away from. What was his inner child trying to tell him? I'm sure his inner child tried so hard to get his attention to invite him on the journey into the unknown, to find his way back home. But clearly he wasn't ready. He just drowned out the whispers until they eventually disappeared.

Adult-me wasn't ready for some time either. I had to wait and be patient. I knew she would come eventually. She almost came a number of years ago whilst on holiday with some friends. Out of the blue she confessed to her friend that she had just had the most peculiar memory pop into her head. The memory was that she had been abused by a family member, but she quickly dismissed it. Clearly, she wasn't ready to take the giant leap to explore this truth, so she shoved it back in the box and poured enough wine over it that, once again, it became temporarily erased from her mind.

The lid remained on the box for quite some time until that day when it finally burst open. It felt so liberating for me to no longer have to hide inside with that box taking up so much room. I was really squashed. Suddenly, with this enormous secret outside of adult-me, there was so much more space inside for me to breathe. I just had to wait until she was ready to find me.

What adult-me had unearthed was truly shocking, and it sent her into a tremendous downward spiral. She felt like she was dying. She was, but in a really good way. I know it didn't seem to her that any part of this experience was good, but I knew this was the start of the journey. This was the end of the veiled version of her, pretending she was just fine. This was the first step of her rebirth. Whilst I hated seeing her look so devastated and lost, I knew it was all part of the process to reconnect with me and to find her way back home. She had to hit rock bottom. I knew she would shatter into a million pieces. But I also knew she would experience the bounce back, and the life that was waiting for her far exceeded the life she had left.

This shocking revelation and its profound tremors had jolted adult-me out of her deep, amnesic sleep. This was her wake-up call. She had ignored all previous attempts, so this time it came with such force that she had no option but to wake up. This is what happens every time we ignore the call. It just gets louder and louder until we are willing to listen. Adult-me had been forced into waking up. She had been presented with a quest that she had to accept. She could not go back to her ordinary world. She had to venture into the woods and face her shadows.

The box had exploded and in the destruction that surrounded her, adult-me spotted something glistening. It was the start of a golden thread. She instinctively knew this was the thread she had to follow to guide her out of this living nightmare. What she didn't realise was this was the thread I had been holding all this time. If she chose to follow it, she would be guided towards me, and together we would venture on this epic journey to RESTORY our lives.

Thankfully, adult-me tentatively picked up the thread and held it in her trembling hand. On it was a message. *'Listen to the niggle and follow the thread.'* Adult-me wanted to laugh at the absurdity of the message. This was not a niggle! This was a detonation! But then it dawned on her that the niggle had been there for quite some time, and she had ignored it. Her body was constantly trying to send her messages, clues, breadcrumbs, but she had discounted each and every one of them. The niggle started out small, but it grew and it grew. Adult-me kept ignoring it until it grew so big it eventually burst out of her. Now she been forced to wake up, she had to accept the realisation.

She followed the thread a little further and uncovered a second message: *Jump into the unknown.* She was being guided to venture forwards even though the path wasn't clear. I wanted her to know that if she waited for the path to be neatly paved before her, she would be waiting forever. It's important you realise this: the path to your healing is never laid out neatly in front of you. It will be dark, messy, uncertain. You just have to take a leap of faith. It is scary leaving your known world, without the clarity of what awaits you. However, the rewards are worth every drop of fear. Have courage and jump into the unknown. Adult-me knew in that moment exactly what she had to do.

STEP 2 – EXPLORE

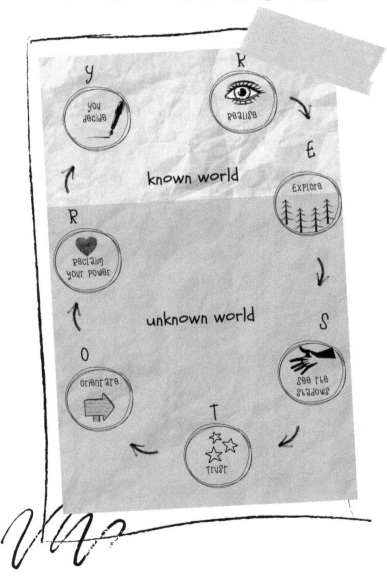

As you stand at the edge of the forest, the path is obscured. Perhaps no path even exists. Maybe it's up to you to forge your own way through the woods. The trees cast shadows on the ground, and you have no idea which way to go. Yet, you continue taking small steps forwards, battling your way through the thorny branches, becoming entangled in the undergrowth. Hitting dead ends is all part of the process. They force us to carve out our own way, not to follow in someone else's footsteps. This is a time to be brave, courageous, and to have faith that the process of transformation will be worth it. Nobody else can do it for you. You have to be willing to take that first step, to cross over the threshold in order to heal and transform.

The woods have always been my happy place. I feel so alive when surrounded by the tall trees and the sunshine pours though the leaves above. It makes everything sparkle and shine like magic. I often see flickers of light dart about from branch to branch. I know people say fairies don't exist, but I still believe in them. My favourite game is to spot faces in the trees. I often see ancient, wise old men in the trunks of the big oak trees and elegant women dancing in the branches of silver birches. They have been there for so many years. They know the truth of the land. My absolute favourite place to sit is at the bottom of an old tree, with my back leaning against the rough bark. The soft moss makes a cushion for me to rest on and I feel so connected to everything around me. It's almost like I can feel the Earth's heart beat in time with my own. I feel safe, secure and connected. I could sit here for hours, but then the forest energy shifts, and I feel afraid.

When the sunlight starts to disappear, a low mist settles, and the trees form giant shadows. That is when I feel like running and hiding. That is when the forest morphs into an unsettling place and not one that I want to go into alone. The sounds always seem so much louder. The branches creek and crack, which makes my heart thump in my chest. I don't know who or what is hiding in there.

But this is all part of the second phase of the journey. Going towards the shadows and facing whatever is there, no matter how terrifying it might be. This is the only way we can fully heal. We have to be brave and face up to whatever is in there. Lots of people try to miss out this bit and go around the edge of the forest. They think that skipping around the forest, simply following love and light will bring about their deepest manifestations. That doesn't work. You have to face the shadows if you want to transform. Think about the caterpillar and the cocoon. The caterpillar has to go into the darkness in order to turn into a beautiful butterfly. It can't just skip that bit and expect to magically wake up one day with beautiful wings.

Going inwards requires courage. We have all heard tales of bloodthirsty wolves skulking through the undergrowth, their bodies seeped with deception and trickery. We have to go into this phase with our eyes wide open. We must remain curious, brave, and be prepared to question the reality in front of us. A cloak of deceit can skew our vision, so we must remain vigilant at all times. This is a time to question, is the wolf indeed a sinister creature, or have our old stories and tales led us to this conclusion? Where in fact does the real danger lie?

The Forest

Dark ominous shadows,
enticing me in.
Waves of anticipation,
prickling my skin.

A sense of wonder and awe,
calling my name,
A warning that life,
will never be the same.

I yearn to discover,
what the dark shadows hide.
Parts of my unconscious,
that have been kept inside.

Yet I'm frozen with fear,
for what truth do they hold?
What if I can't face
the answers I'm told?

The branches reach out,
they wrap around me.
Drawing me deeper,
I can no longer flee.

I've journeyed too far,
there's no going back.
I'm lost in the woods,
With no path or track.

It's time to be curious,
willing to learn.
Uncover the answers,
I so desperately yearn.

These parts of me,
have been buried so deep.
They've caused me such pain,
and made me weep.

Yet I discover these shadows,
are actually my guide.
If I follow their knowledge,
a path opens wide.

Urging me forwards,
Through the labyrinth of my mind.
To become whole again,
Connected, aligned.

Step into the woods,
lean into the fear.
Trust my path home,
will suddenly become clear.

The trees hold such wisdom,
rooted to the earth.
Supporting me fully,
as I begin my rebirth.

Adult-me was bewildered in the middle of the forest. She had completely lost her way, and she had no idea what to do. She felt trapped in a cycle of self-doubt. The forest was dense, thick, full of dark, twisted trees and thorny branches. She had become entangled, her whole body ensnared in the confusion. Her skin had been pricked with the sharp jagged edges of the memories she was uncovering. She was hurting deeply but couldn't escape. She had to face up to the truth that the memories held.

Day after day, adult-me battled through this suffocating underworld, gasping for breath. She kept asking herself, 'Why have these memories surfaced now? What if they aren't true? Surely, I would remember? What if I have made them up?' These unanswerable questions taunted her day and night. She was so confused as to why now, after all these years, these intrusive thoughts would suddenly appear in her head. Flashbacks of images that make her body convulse in horror, but her mind seemingly deny. Snippets of revolting phrases floating around in her head, apparently disconnected yet equally disturbingly familiar. Her mind told her she was going mad. Yet her body responded with a deep remembering that sent shivers down her spine.

She frantically wished she understood what was going on inside her head. She was frozen in fear and couldn't access the key to open up the answers to her own confusion. The truth was she had held the key for years. She had created a whole business around the very thing that she was desperately trying to understand. The years leading up to this shocking revelation were dedicated to teaching children about the brain and how it functions when experiencing stress.

In this moment of distress, she had frozen, and in doing so, she could no longer access the information about brain theory she already knew so well. If she could allow herself to pause and breathe, she would understand why she had blocked out these memories from her childhood.

I did wonder why she decided to create a wellbeing business for children. I think deep down, without realising it, she was trying to help me, her inner child. She didn't know that at the time, of course, but it made sense to me. Anyway, I am very thankful that she taught thousands of children over the years, because I was listening every time. She clearly explained how the brain works and now I will explain it to you, the same way she taught me.

The brain is very complicated, but we are discovering more and more about how it functions, particularly when we are faced with stress. She taught me that there are three key parts of the brain that are important in understanding what happens when we are faced with potential threat or danger. I will now explain what had happened in her brain all those years ago and why she couldn't remember, until decades later.

This is the brain simplified into three key areas. The amygdala (the monkey), the hippocampus (the elephant), and the pre-frontal cortex (the owl).

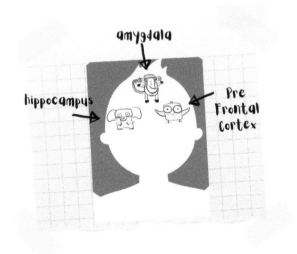

We all have a monkey (amygdala), in fact we actually have two, one on each side of the brain. The monkey is responsible for detecting fear and preparing our body for an emergency response. It is like our internal alarm centre, which keeps us safe. This part of our brain is very reactive, and whenever it feels under threat of any kind, it will send a signal to the rest of the body to either run away, fight the threat, or freeze. When our amygdala has been activated, we are in a state of fear and we cannot think of anything else. All our attention and focus is on survival. We may notice physical changes such as sweaty palms or an increased heart rate. Our breathing becomes more shallow and rapid as we prepare our bodies to run away if we have to.

Working alongside the monkey is the elephant (hippocampus). The elephant's job is to hold onto important memories from the past. The hippocampus takes our short-term memories and files them away permanently in a long-term storage filing cabinet. These memories record how people, places, smells and sounds made us feel. This is why when we smell cinnamon biscuits baking in the oven, we are immediately reminded of Christmas. The elephant stores this information and if it is necessary will warn the monkey to react.

An example of how monkey and elephant can work together is if you see a dog tied up outside a shop and you go to stroke it. Suddenly the dog, turns towards you, starts barking really loudly, and is baring his sharp teeth. Your monkey will immediately react to the perceived danger and will release waves of adrenaline and cortisol through your body so you can respond accordingly. In this case you will probably run away even though the dog is tied up. Your elephant will then store that information about dogs in his great big filing cabinet of memories. Then, the next time you spot a dog, even if it is a really gentle, soft, playful puppy, the elephant will warn your monkey, and your immediate reaction will be to run away. These brain functions are essential for keeping us safe when real danger is present, and if we didn't have them, we would probably not survive for very long. Imagine if instead of a dog, we had encountered a poisonous snake. We would need the quick reactions of monkey and elephant to keep us safe.

The third part of the brain is the owl (Pre-frontal cortex). The owl is required to make logical and rational decisions. It helps us to communicate, organise and problem-solve. Our PFC isn't fully developed until we are grown up (around 25 – 28 years old), so remember that the next time you are trying to rationalise with a child. We don't have the ability to see things entirely logically like you grown-ups. The other important thing to remember about the owl is that it can only work when the monkey is quiet.

If our monkey starts to get all agitated and jumpy, then the owl will simply fly away. This is why when we feel stressed or threatened in any way, we react without thinking logically first, even if we are not in any life or death situation. Monkey is great when we need to escape real danger because it helps us to react quickly. But most days we are safe, yet our monkeys are still on high alert. Many of us can find ourselves flooded by the stress chemicals when someone has said something mean to us, when someone ignores us or if someone has pushed in front of us in a queue. I'm sure you can think of numerous examples when your monkey has taken over and your owl has flown away.

So, what does all this all have to do with my adult self's memory loss?

These three parts of the brain all play an important role in regulating our emotions and responding to fear. After emotional trauma, these areas may not function fully effectively. The amygdala can become hyperactive. Often a person who has experienced something traumatic will be sensitive to other stimuli, and can be triggered more easily, which can lead to increased levels of anxiety. The hippocampus can also become physically affected following trauma and can actually reduce in size. This means the elephant will become smaller and therefore less effective at storing the memories. Memory loss is a natural survival mechanism that we develop to protect ourselves from psychological trauma. An experience of sexual abuse can lead to dissociative amnesia, which is a helpful survival coping mechanism. This memory loss can continue until a time when the person feels ready to handle the memory. Often, when these memories are suppressed, when they begin to resurface there is no logical order. All that is left is disconnected images, sounds and sensations in the body.

This is what happened to me around the age of eight. My monkey would have probably become extremely agitated, my owl would have flown away, and my elephant would have stopped working properly. They all did a great job of protecting me by not holding onto the memories. It's like I just went away to some other place. But where did I go? I don't have the answers. I wish I did. Wherever I went, so too did most of my memories and this makes me sad.

I am thankful that my monkey, owl and elephant helped me out during this time. I was probably not be able to actually physically run away or hide from what was happening to me, but I was able to 'go away' someplace in my head. When I try to think back, it feels like my body was still there, but my mind had gone. I had floated away. Sometimes, I get flashbacks of tracing the lines in between the bathroom tiles and make a road map of all the cracks. I seemed to be able to disappear off into a world inside my own head whilst my body stayed and endured the bad stuff.

The other part of me that had become really good at wearing a mask, was able to carry on pretending everything was ok. That version of me seemed ok to the outside world. However, it wasn't the whole me. It was a fake, coping strategy part of me that was very good at performing and showing that world that I was a good girl. The real part of me that had the horrible feelings was locked away and filled with shame. That part was where I was left to hide and this was where I had been hiding all that time, waiting to be found so that I could once again reconnect with adult-me. But adult-me was lost.

She was desperately trying to find her way through the undergrowth of the forest. Logically, she knew how the brain functions, but she could not possibly believe it all to be true. She was lost in the confusion of her own mind. She wanted to hide from the world. The trees had wrapped their gnarly, leafless branches around her quivering body, whispering the secrets they had held on to for decades. The chaos of the tangled tree roots from her unconscious mind had knotted and twisted their way into her present. Every few steps she tentatively took forwards she found herself once again trapped in the confusion of the unknown landscape. Everything felt unfamiliar and she was continuously hitting dead ends. The tree roots erupted from the earth, tripping her up. She fell, landing sharply on the ground. As she lay here on the forest floor, she was aware of the dark shadows looming over her. She had two choices. Turn back and run as fast as she could to her known world and lock this secret away with more alcohol and more pretending. Or face up to whatever was threatening to reveal itself.

She rested against the trunk of an old oak tree and felt the soft cushioning of the velvety moss comfort her. Despite the harsh conditions of the dark forest, she was reminded that she was not alone. She felt the pulse of the trees' lifeforce, willing her to keep going. The trees had seen it all. They have stood strong and weathered all storms. They had been the constant in the decades of chaos. As she paused and breathed in the earthy scent of the fallen leaves, she was once again reminded that she was the hero on her journey, not the victim. Here on the forest floor, she chose to continue pushing onwards on this agonising path. She knew it would rip her open, but she knew eventually the wounds would heal. One day they would become scars, forever depicting the trail of her courageous healing journey. She knew she must remain open to the discovery before her. She knew she must find courage and curiosity to keep surging forwards, questioning, no longer accepting life is it is. She needed answers. She needed to unveil the deceit. She was prepared to keep fighting.

As she picked herself up from the forest floor, she uncovered the next part of the golden thread and read its message: *Make friends with your shadow* side. She wanted to run away from her shadows, but they had so much to teach her. Our shadows are here to guide us. I was trying to remind adult-me that she had to face the darkness before she could bring out the light.

STEP 3 –
SEE THE SHADOWS

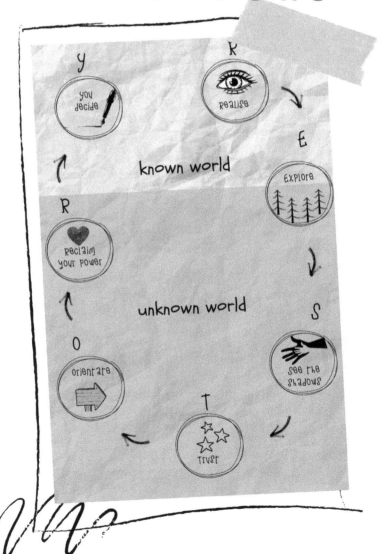

see the
shadows

This phase of the journey requires you to open yourself up to your shadow side. This is not a time to hold it all together, to remain strong, to paint a brave face on. This is a time to remove the brave face and to allow the truth of your soul to show up in the world. Allow the tears to fall as they will help to wash away the pain. By releasing everything you have repressed, you are able to remember who you really are. This is the time to surrender, to soften to crack yourself open. Once the dense fog lifts, the light will shine once more, creating fresh new growth, a abundance of new opportunities. Feel the beat of you heart and remember who you are, who you have alwa been.

Adult-me stood up and placed her quivering hands on the nearby tree trunk. She steadied her breath and glanced around her. The moonlight had cast vast shadows on the forest floor. The shapes of the trees' spindly branches morphed into unidentified objects. Her heart beat loudly. In that moment she had such gratitude for the fullness of the moon, as it was her only companion in the oppressive darkness. Its presence spilling out possibilities in the maze of impenetrable obscurity.

She knew she had to go through this next phase and face her own shadows. She had spent so long running away from them that she had to find courage to go in and see what was there. We so often want to control, fight and force our way into the light, but this will not work. We have to allow the shadows to crack us open and let all the dark emotions out. No matter how ugly, shameful and disgusting they are, they have to be seen, heard and given space. Remember they have been shoved into that box for so long. They never went away; they just got bigger and bigger, angrier and angrier, darker and darker. Whatever the emotion was when you first shoved it in, I can guarantee it is a million times bigger now. How do I know? Remember, I had been locked inside adult-me right next to that box. I have heard it moaning and groaning, threatening to spill open. I have seen the distraction techniques that adult-me attempted to keep it shut. They don't work. They might silence it for a while, maybe even years, but one day it has to open, and the contents have to spill out, if you ever want to feel whole again. You cannot feel whole, complete, and fulfilled if you still have an unopened box bursting at the seams with buried emotions.

Adult-me had no idea where she was. She was lost in the depths of the forest. She was acutely aware of the cracking of twigs and dead leaves underfoot. A smell of trepidation hung in the air. She didn't recognise anything anymore. Her whole world had been tipped upside down.

She knew she couldn't go back to life as it was before, pretending everything was ok. She had uncovered this colossal secret, and she had to understand more. Even though she was confused, gripped by heartache and terrified, she kept stepping one foot in front of the other. She could feel her heart rate increase as she navigated her way through these unknown parts of her mind. The sounds were unfamiliar, and they kept her on high alert. She felt anxious, panic-stricken and tangled in amongst the web of bewilderment.

As the leaves danced in the cold breeze overhead, adult-me fell to her knees and wept. I watched her, as she was submerged by each wave of emotion that oozed out from her box. It was devastating to see that part of me hurting so deeply, but I knew it was the most important part of the healing process.

As the mist fell and adult-me lay strewn on the moon-lit ground, amongst the decomposing detritus of the forest floor, she realised she was about to face the next layer of the healing process. The old woman rumoured to linger in the shadows of the forest had found her limp body and dragged her into a cold, empty cave. The heaviness was so oppressive adult-me could barely breathe. The old woman had been prowling the forest, waiting for the right moment to capture her prey.

In my fairy tales, the old woman was often referred to as the Wicked Witch. She was the old crone who has lived in the forest since time began. People have feared her for centuries as she was potent, all knowing, all seeing. The old woman had the ability to morph into whatever shadow form you needed to see and hear the messages she held. For adult-me she had morphed into a Wicked Witch, much like the one featured in Hansel and Gretal. One that was intent on destroying adult-me. She was that horrid, nasty part of her being that spoke to her in such a malicious and spiteful way. She was her inner critic that beat her up when she was feeling sad, kicked her in the guts when she was in pain, laughed in her face when she felt humiliated, tormented her, convinced her she was worthless. The Witch inside of adult-me was very familiar and deeply embroiled in eroding any remnants of self-respect that adult-me once had.

Adult-me found herself locked inside the Witch's cage, deep in the womb of the cave. The cold numbed her face and crept under her clothes, seeping into every inch of her body. The Witch's cackle ricocheted off the stony walls. Echoes of spitefulness resonated around her as the Witch triumphantly glowered into her cauldron, her finger trailing in the noxious fluid. This time, she has succeeded. She had gained the upper hand and discovered the key to her victim's fragility. She tunnelled her way through the dying fragments of my adult-self's resolve, eating away at any final morsels of self-respect. Watching my adult-self collapse in despair fuelled her to keep goading, keep poking, even though adult-me could barely breathe.

The Witch's blood ran thick with spite and malevolence, and she did not stop, even though the tears poured down my adult self's streaked cheeks. The Witch took this as a signal to step up the assault. She increased the volume of the taunts and jeers.

You are disgusting. You deserve to rot in the putrid pus of decomposing waste. That's where you belong. You are rotten to the core. This is exactly what you deserve. You are bad, so very bad.

If I were you, I'd just die now. You do not deserve to live. You are despicable. Totally unworthy of love. Who in their right mind would love you if they really knew what you really were? You have always been vile, revolting and filthy. You deserve to rot in hell.

This voice was with her both day and night. Even when she was at her lowest point, it continued stabbing at her. Adult-me knew deep down that the abuse happened, as she could feel it permeate every cell in her body. Everything about her suddenly made sense. It was like the missing jigsaw piece had been slotted into place. However, the fear of self-doubt was overbearing.

She was so confused and traumatised to have these memories surface and she was at a loss as to what to do with them. Again, and again, she questioned her memories because she didn't want to believe they were true. She was deeply anguished by these thoughts, and on dark days she thought she must be crazy. She desperately wanted these terrible memories to never have appeared in her mind. But they had. They had erupted out of her, ripping her apart, destroying everything she had ever known or believed to be true of her childhood.

Whilst she had found the courage to share her anguish with her husband and she was eternally grateful for his unwavering support, she was terrified of sharing this horror with her family in Wales. The abuser was still very much part of their lives and she was extremely fearful of what their reaction would be. She knew she had no choice but to speak her truth. This was too big to remain concealed from them. Plus, she desperately needed their support.

She finally found the courage to tell her family in Wales. They were understandably appalled to hear adult-me disclose that she had recalled memories of being sexually abused as a child. Nobody wanted to hear the monstrous words that there was an abuser in the fold, yet for some relatives, it didn't seem to come as a huge surprise. The well-respected roles this individual held in society, coupled with his access to children, mirrored that of other convicted abusers. There was also a feeling that there was something about him that made others uncomfortable.

Whilst nobody explicitly pinpointed what gave them that feeling, a couple of relatives stated they had always felt uneasy in his company, as he emitted an energy that 'gave them the creeps.'

For others in the family, the suggestion that adult-me had been abused by this relative was utterly ludicrous. The prospect that there was incest present in the family was considered completely absurd. They couldn't believe that a 'respectable person in society' could be an abuser. Everything adult-me had been dreading, began to play out in front of her. She had been so afraid to speak her truth for fear that she wouldn't be believed. These words seemed to run deep within her. They seemed worryingly familiar: 'No one will believe you.'

Those family members she needed more than ever, were unable to hear her truth. Their own defence mechanisms kicked in and they began to blame her for ruining their lives. She was now deemed responsible for bringing this heinous accusation into the family. Adult-me was experiencing the often-commonplace DARVO response of Deny, Attack, and Reverse Victim and Offender. They were so appalled by these accusations and their ramifications, that they had to deny the abuse ever happened. They started to attack adult-me for disclosing. They were the victims as their lives were being torn apart. Adult-me was deemed the offender. It was heart-wrenching. Adult-me was left all alone, crushed by guilt and feeling responsible for the distress she was seemingly causing her family. The Wicked Witch inside her feasted on this grief. It fuelled the vicious onslaught of self-loathing.

These family members were so distraught by the accusations, they were intent on finding any explanation for what was unfolding. They couldn't and wouldn't accept that the abuse had happened. They had to find evidence to prove the accusations were untrue. Their research led them to the only possible explanation – in their eyes. According to them, adult-me was clearly suffering with 'false memory syndrome'.

Hearing these words stabbed adult-me hard in the heart. She was utterly distraught to have these memories in her head in the first place. She just wanted to be held and soothed and reassured that all was going to be ok. But instead, she was accused of lying. According to her family she was making the whole thing up.

Adult-me decided to research 'false memory syndrome' and was aghast at what she found. This so-called syndrome was created by accused parents who founded a non-profit organisation in Philadelphia. They invested millions of dollars to promote a false memory defence for themselves. Founding members, Pamela and Peter Freyd, created the False Memory Syndrome Foundation (FMSF) after their daughter, Professor Jennifer Freyd, accused her father of sexually abusing her when she was a child. Jennifer was in her thirties when she began to recall her childhood memories of abuse. Jennifer's mother, Pamela, publicly contested the accusation. The fact that Jennifer's account of abuse was supported by her sister and her uncle was deemed irrelevant. Peter and Pamela Freyd were joined by other parents similarly confronted by their children of abuse, and the 'false memory' PR campaign was underway.

When adult-me first heard about 'false memory syndrome', she thought it sounded like a very scientific diagnosis, but it turns out it is not a scientifically researched condition at all. Apparently, the FMSF explained on their website how they came up with the name. '...*Since the parents were convinced that what their children thought were memories were really incorrect beliefs, the term "false memory" seemed appropriate.*'

Adult-me was shocked to discover that the media continued to report on this campaign, alleging that there was supposedly an epidemic of 'false memory syndrome'. This powerful sounding 'syndrome', which was fabricated by accused parents and had no scientific backing, was being used to discredit the testimonies of so many people.

The more adult-me started to research this organisation, the more shocked and appalled she was. Psychologist Elizabeth Loftus, who was a board member of the FMSF, had been quoted as saying that her own experience of molestation was *not that big a deal*'. She was a so-called expert on false memories, yet she had no clinical or research experience working with sexual abuse survivors.

She had been quoted in the Los Angeles Times as saying, '*The world is full of people who support accusers. I think people who are accused deserve some modicum of support as well.*' She had made a successful career as an expert witness testifying in the defence of clients including Ted Bundy (American serial killer and rapist known to have killed at least 36 women in the 1970s), Jerry Sandusky (football coach convicted on 45 counts of child sexual abuse), and Harvey Weinstein (American film producer and convicted sex offender).

In her testimony in the Harvey Weinstein trial, she explained how false memories could be implanted and believed, citing the 'Lost in the Mall' study as evidence. On numerous occasions, Loftus had cited that study and had claimed '*about a quarter of people*' can be made to believe false memories that are externally implanted. Adult-me decided to research more about Loftus' study.

Loftus had stated '*At some point, I came up with the idea: Why don't we try to make people believe and remember that they were lost in a shopping mall – that they were frightened and crying and ultimately rescued and reunited with their* family?' Loftus carried out the study with 24 subjects. 'Each participant was provided with a booklet containing brief accounts of three true childhood incidents which were provided by a relative. Relatives also provided 'information about a *plausible* shopping trip to a mall or large department store' so that a fourth false incident that supposedly occurred when the participant and close family member were together, could be included in the booklet (Loftus & Pickrell, 1995, p. 721). 'Participants were told that they were participating in a study on childhood memories, and that [the researchers] were interested in how and why people remembered some things and not others. They were asked to complete the booklets by reading what their relative had told [the researchers] about each event, and then writing what they remembered about each event. If they did not remember the event, they were told to write '*I do not remember this*'.' (Loftus & Pickrell, 1995, p. 722)

In the results of the study, the authors claimed, nineteen subjects correctly identified getting lost in the mall was not the real memory. Only five subjects '*fully or partially*' believed the false memory. This result led to Loftus stating that '*about a quarter or people*' can be made to believe false memories that are externally implanted.

There were parts of this study that didn't feel right to adult-me. The fact that the subjects were asked to recall a memory of being lost in a mall felt entirely different to recalling a memory of abuse. Most children, at some point in their lives have lost sight of their parent of guardian in a supermarket or shopping centre and therefore this memory is a plausible one. This was explored further by Pezdek in 1995 in a similar study which found that 3 out of 20 participants recalled a plausible false memory of getting lost in a shopping mall, however none of the participants accepted an implausible false memory that they had received a painful enema as a child from their parent. This seemed to make more sense to adult-me.

Remembering receiving a painful enema or being sexually abused by a family member is not akin to remembering getting lost in a shopping centre. Adult-me was struggling to come to terms with the validity of this study. This study was being cited in court cases such as that of Harvey Weinstein. These were also the 'scientific facts' that had underpinned her own family's beliefs that her memories of abuse were false.

If that wasn't enough, another founding member of the FMSF, Ralph Underwager was also a prolific defence expert for people accused of child sexual abuse. He was quoted in Paidika: The Journal of Paedophilia as saying: *'Paedophiles can boldly and courageously affirm what they choose. They can say that what they want is to find the best way to love. I am also a theologian and as a theologian, I believe it is God's will that there be closeness and intimacy, unity of the flesh, between people. A paedophile can say: 'This closeness is possible for me within the choices that I've made.'*

The interview quite rightly caused huge controversy and Underwager resigned from the FMSF's scientific advisory board.

Adult-me was finding it really difficult to understand how her family in Wales chose to believe this Foundation. The FMSF dissolved in December 2019, but unfortunately the damage had already been done. Thanks to their repeated claims over 30 years, adult-me was being accused of suffering with false memories. It seemed to make sense to her family that a therapist must have implanted these false memories into my adult-self's head. In their eyes, there could be no other possible explanation. They were convinced adult-me had received 'recovered memory therapy' and these memories had been implanted by some rogue therapist.

Adult-me had never had 'recovered memory therapy'.

What's more, adult-me wasn't even receiving any therapy when these memories surfaced. They came to her without any hypnosis or guided imagery. Nobody had suggested them to her. She remembered on her own. One summer's afternoon, whilst chatting to a friend about the chronic tightness in her jaw, these disturbing memories catapulted themselves into the forefront of her mind, with a terrifying familiarity. Out of the blue she clearly recalled standing in the bathroom as a child, whilst this family member touched her naked body. She had flashes of memory of being touched by him in both her family home and in the home of her abuser. She had clear images of him unzipping his brown trousers. The words 'lick it like a lollipop' circulated in her mind. The memories were fragmented. The memories were deeply disturbing. The memories were horrifyingly familiar.

Adult-me was determined to find answers about her abuser. When adult-me started to ask and question other family members, she soon realised her efforts were futile. Sadly, it seemed that any relatives who had suspicions about her abuser were also branded as insane. Some months before adult-me recalled her memories of abuse, a relative had actually referred to the abuser as a 'paedophile'. Unsurprisingly that particular family member was regarded to be 'narcissistic and should never be trusted'. It seemed anybody who dared to state the truth behind the abuse was branded as a liar and untrustworthy. Protecting the family reputation was clearly the main priority.

Adult-me was beginning to realise that some people were simply not able to look at the awful truth. They did not possess the willingness to accept that sexual abuse was perpetrated within the family. It was easier to maintain alliances with the abuser because they could turn away from any uncomfortable truths and difficult feelings being stirred up. It was easier to turn a blind eye, and to label any accusations as crazy and insane.

Adult-me was hurting deeply and felt rejected and abandoned. She was extremely scared and concerned. Whilst she knew she wasn't suffering with 'false memory' she was terrified that she was perhaps insane. How could she have a repressed memory for so long? Surely this only happened to crazy people?

In an attempt to calm her anxieties, she requested a session with a psychiatrist to try to understand if she was indeed losing her mind. She researched thoroughly to find an experienced professional who would be able to identify if she was in fact somehow fabricating these memories and had indeed gone mad. Her session was with a consultant forensic psychiatrist who had worked in a wide range of clinical and criminal justice settings. He also had experience of working with women with personality disorders in a non-secure mental health unit.

The psychiatrist written report stated, *'Katie spent the hour-long appointment going through the memories she has experienced relating to the suspected abuse. Katie understands that I am not in a position to establish on her behalf whether or not the abuse took place although I did acknowledge that her description does not appear to be inconsistent with the experiences of a child who has undergone sexual abuse.'*

Hearing these words come from a consultant psychiatrist was so reassuring and made the Wicked Witch inside of adult-me, quieten her assault a little. Encouraged by this step forward, and with a slight pause in the Witch's taunts and goads, adult-me started to research repressed memories and found some very encouraging information. Researcher and professor Jennifer Freyd, the daughter of the founders of the FMSF, explained that survivors can repress their memory of abuse completely until a time in their lives when it is safe enough to remember – and even then, memories often emerge in non-narrative forms such as emotional responses to triggers, physical sensations, intrusive images, etc.

This made complete sense as what she was remembering was not a chronological, orderly, structured sequence of events, but random, distressing memories, and visceral reactions to certain types of music and sounds.

She then read articles written by Michael Salter, a professor of criminal psychology, who states, 'About one third of child sexual abuse survivors will experience partial or full amnesia for their abuse.' He said:

This amnesia or delayed recall has multiple sources. As children, they may have dissociated or gone 'blank' to cope with their abuse. Shameful feelings prompt many children to avoid thinking about the abuse at all. Children may not know that what happened was abusive due to the manipulations of the perpetrators. All of these processes disrupt memory encoding and recall. In adulthood, survivors may then encounter triggers that remind them of the abuse and find themselves recalling childhood events that they were previously unaware of. This process is often profoundly distressing and destabilizing. The return of these memories is a common reason for abuse survivors to seek mental health care.

- Renee Fabian, 'Survivors Celebrate the End of the False Memory Syndrome Foundation After 27 Years', The Mighty website (2019).

What Michael Salter described was exactly what had happened to adult-me, and she finally started to feel wave after wave of relief that she wasn't going mad. Each wave that washed over her, once more quietened the Witch. Encouraged by her progress, she sought further therapy to support her in this heart-wrenching situation. She began EMDR therapy (Eye Movement Desensitization and Reprocessing), which is a psychotherapy treatment designed to alleviate the distress associated with traumatic memories. Gradually, as she started to come to terms with the trauma, she was able to process the impact it had on her and her body.

The stress in the body was of particular interest. Bessel van der Kolk's book *The Body Keeps the Score* proved extremely helpful in her recovery, and the following passages made complete sense to her:

Long after a traumatic experience is over, it may be reactivated at the slightest hint of danger and mobilize disturbed brain circuits and secrete massive amounts of stress hormones. This precipitates unpleasant emotions, intense physical sensations, and impulsive and aggressive actions. These posttraumatic reactions feel incomprehensible and overwhelming. Feeling out of control, survivors of trauma often begin to fear that they are damaged to the core and beyond redemption. P. 2

Traumatized people chronically feel unsafe inside their bodies: The past is alive in the form of gnawing interior discomfort. Their bodies are constantly bombarded by visceral warning signs, and, in an attempt to control these processes, they often become expert at ignoring their gut feelings and in numbing awareness of what is played out inside. They learn to hide from their selves. P 96

Traumatised people are often afraid of feeling. It is not so much the perpetrators but their own physical sensations that are now the enemy. Apprehension about being hijacked by uncomfortable sensations keeps the body frozen and the mind shut. Even though trauma is a thing of the past, the emotional brain keeps generating sensations that make the sufferer feel scared and helpless. P208

– Dr. Bessel van der Kolk, *The Body Keeps the Score*

Adult-me couldn't believe the words she was reading. They seemed to describe her experience exactly. How could she be mad if one of the world's leading experts on post-traumatic stress was describing her own experience of how her trauma was affecting her brain, body and nervous system?

The words 'damaged to the core' were the exact words the Witch had used in her assault. Everything about this body of work seemed so familiar, so accurate in describing how she had felt for so long.

The 'gnawing interior discomfort' was exactly what my adult-self felt. She had learned to hide from herself whilst carrying around this shameful, invisible secret. For so many years, she had been filled with anxiety, often on edge and jumpy. She regularly had intrusive thoughts, such as if someone was late, she'd panic and convince herself that they must have gotten into a car crash. She would constantly hear creaking noises in the house and think someone was there. She didn't feel safe in her own body and would frequently zone out to avoid the discomfort. She froze when her body was lovingly caressed by her husband. She felt pure rage burst out of her when she heard music from the 1980s. Now she understood why.

Reading this work, combined with her own research on both the FMSF and recovered memories, led her to the conclusion that she was not crazy. She was in fact experiencing a horrific trauma, further impacted by her family's response. These painful emotions had been stuck inside her for so long, but she knew she had to release them. She had to face the Wicked Witch and hear every single word to had to say. She was no longer afraid of this wretched part of her being.

She invited the Witch to sit with her and let out the remains of her vicious opinions. She allowed herself to surrender to the hurtful words. She allowed these spiteful judgements to be voiced and then asked herself, Are they true? The Wicked Witch may claim she is a bad person, rotten to the core, but is she? Are there any facts to suggest this to be actually correct?

As she questioned each of these beliefs the Wicked Witch had about her, she was gradually able to see that they weren't true. She wasn't bad. These feelings were drenched in shame. But she realised the shame wasn't hers. It belonged to her abuser. She was aware of the constant sense of guilt that she carried around with her for years. This guilt didn't belong to her. It belonged to her abuser. The abuser was vile, rotten to the core. He deserved to be locked away, not her.

Whilst she desperately didn't want to believe the abuse happened, she knew in her entire body it was true. She began to surrender to the truth and started to accept what had happened to her when she was just a child. She didn't have clear, chronological memories of her abuse, but her body knew that it was holding onto this hidden secret. It had wormed its way through her cells, holding onto the shame, hiding it from herself. Her recurring migraines and her chronic jaw pain were both clear physical signs that she was holding on to something. But now the truth had surfaced, and she didn't have to hold on anymore.

The Witch's Cage

Trapped in despair,
afraid and alone.
Feeling so scared,
so far from home.

Suffering torment,
all through the night,
I can no longer bear it,
I've lost the fight.

Damaged, broken,
sick to the core.
Worthless, empty,
a heap on the floor.

Self–loathing permeates,
through to my bones.
Listening to the Witch,
her rasping moans.

Facing this atrocity,
fills me with shame.
Traumatic emotions,
Too harrowing to name.

The sharpness of sorrow,
as they accuse me of lying.
Twisting the knife in me,
I'm slowly dying.

Turning their backs,
in my hour of need.
Ignoring my cries,
as I desperately plead.

I'm scared, I'm lost,
I wish it would end.
Their denial of me,
I just can't comprehend.

Do I deserve,
to be treated like this?
Abandoned, rejected,
into the dark abyss.

Rotten, revolting,
I fall to my knees.
'Help me' I whisper,
they ignore my pleas.

As I lie on the ground,
racked with despair.
I have no choice,
but to lay myself bare.

It's time to surrender,
to the Witch's cries.
But are they true?
Or are they simply just lies?

Allowing the pain,
to pour out of my soul.
Purging deeply,
from the depths of this hole.

I question the Witch,
are these thoughts really true?
And then in that moment,
the answers I knew.

They belong to my abuser,
They don't belong to me.
As the shadow recedes
I am finally set free.

Adult-me surrendered to the Witch's torment, and in doing so, the daggers of hatred started to lessen their grip. The shadows no longer dominated her. She was not held captive inside of these dark thoughts. The Witch that had been such an oppressive energy had actually served as one of her greatest teachers. By surrendering to the shadows and allowing the Witch to be heard, she was able to uncover her own truth. Adult-me saw the Witch for what she really was: a wise old woman who had, in fact, guided her to trust her intuition, trust her body and trust her innate wisdom. This spark of relief ignited a flicker of light from the depths of the cave.

It started out as a faint glow, but gradually it grew in strength and soon shone so brightly it illuminated the whole cage where adult-me had been trapped. When the light reached into the darkest corner, she uncovered a tear-stained face of a little girl. Adult-me could barely believe it. All this time she had been locked in the cage, listening to the Witch's assault, there was this little girl cowering in the corner. How long had she been there?

That scared little girl was me. Adult-me had finally found me, her inner child. I initially felt apprehensive. I wasn't sure how adult-me would respond. I looked unloved. Dirt was smeared on my face, my clothes were torn and old. I was worried she would turn her back on me, ashamed of what truths I held. But adult-me gently approached me and reassured me that everything was going to be ok. She told me that I was now safe. She soothed my silent cries and wiped away the tears as they trickled down my stained face. I had been trapped inside for so long, the light hurt my eyes. My bare feet ached for reassurance as I tentatively stepped forward.

My adult-self wrapped her arms around my fragile little body and filled me with a love so deep that it infiltrated every fibre of my being. In that moment we merged into one. I finally felt safe. It was the most wonderful feeling. I was able to let go of the fear that my body held on to. I knew that I would no longer be trapped in the confines of this putrid lair.

We allowed the waves of emotion to consume us, as we reconnected after so many decades of being separated. In this warm, comforting, sacred space, the reality really started to hit home. Adult-me knew she was not a bad person. She knew she was not rotten to the core. She was not to blame. It was not her fault. She did nothing wrong. A bad thing had happened to her, but she was not bad. She had no more shame to carry inside of her. It was as if all that rancidity that had been coursing through her veins, was now being squeezed out like pus erupting from an infected wound. She was not a vile person. She was, in fact, a brave, courageous, loving individual who had experienced a heinous trauma.

My adult-self took hold of my trembling hand and together we made our escape. The old woman had left the door to the cage wide open, encouraging us to leave and journey onwards. Finally, I had been released from my confinement. I was no longer trapped inside. I was free. Adult-me had faced her shadows, surrendered to her truth and it had set me free.

As we clambered out of the darkness of the cave, we emerged into the forest. It took a while for our eyes to adjust to the brightness of our reality. The midday sun shone down, and it illuminated the next part of the thread: *Listen to your gut instinct. Trust your intuition, it never lies.* This is what I had been trying to tell adult-me for so long. Her gut knew what her head hadn't yet figured out. In softening and opening herself up to trust she would continue to find freedom.

STEP 4 – TRUST

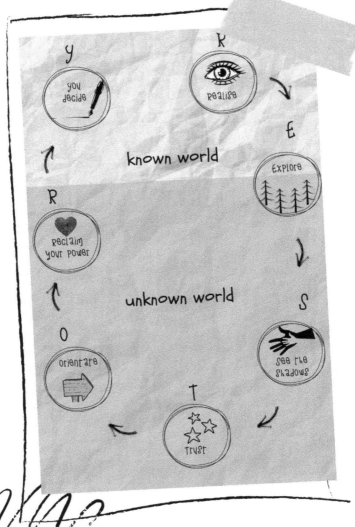

When the mind is playing tricks and stirring up doubt and fear, it's time to conquer it with trust.

Trust your intuition. Trust your gut. Trust your inner child. Your inner child is the only one who was there. They know where the answers can be found.

When faced with fear, choose love, every time. When love is present there is no space for fear. Love your inner child — they have been surrounded by fear for too long. It's time to fill them up with a love so deep they can let go and trust that they are completely held.

I was so excited for the next phase of the journey, as I was now free. I could run and jump and sing and shout. It felt incredible to finally be out of the cage. For a moment I believed this was it and we were now able to live happily ever after. I thought that we had completed the quest and we were on our way back home.

But that's the trouble with the forest. There are tricksters lurking in the least likely of places. Even if you think you are on a path home, you may suddenly find yourself facing a dead end or a twisted path that leads back to where you were previously. The forest is a labyrinth, and it continues to throw tests at you.

Adult-me had come so far. She had faced the Witch, made friends with her shadows, and explored her fears, yet she wasn't completely free. She was experiencing the creeping, suffocating effects of self-doubt. It clambers on you when you are least expecting it and wraps itself around your throat, constricting your every breath. Adult-me would have a period of good days, feeling like she was making progress, then all of a sudden, she would be suffocated by an onslaught of these poisonous vines, squeezing out her strength and courage. These patterns had been part of her for decades. There were not going to go away without a fight.

To protect herself from these poisonous vines, adult-me found refuge in an old derelict castle. She ensured the thick walls were built up as high as possible, keeping her protected from the relentless self-doubt. As we know from our history books, castles were designed to defend and keep people out, and this one was no different. In her fear and confusion, she locked herself away from the pain, but in doing so, she also locked out any prospect of help. This felt right as she still didn't feel worthy.

She was still struggling to accept that she didn't somehow

deserve this. She was trying to release decades worth of shame and found viewing herself with kindness and compassion extremely difficult to access. She could see me, her wounded inner child in that light, but she found accepting her adult-self extremely challenging. She didn't want anyone near her. Even though her husband and close friends were trying to support her, she had pulled up the drawbridge and locked herself away. She felt like she deserved it all. Once locked away in her cold, desolate castle, she wanted to throw away the key and allow herself to disappear.

There have been so many examples over the years when adult-me retreated to the isolation of the castle, cutting herself off from love and support. When she reflected on her life, she sometimes fell into the trap of thinking it was all her fault, that she was such a bad person that she was only worthy of bad things happening to her. She often wondered if it was somehow her own fault that her parents got divorced, and that she somehow contributed to the years of bitter resentment that followed. She carried guilt from her father's demise into his alcoholism. When she was on the receiving end of one of his vicious drunken phone calls in the middle of the night, being called a c**t, she felt she must deserve to be spoken to like that. She felt like she was to blame when he eventually drank himself to death at the age of 51. When the following year her stepdad died suddenly on a walking holiday, she was consumed by more self-loathing. Of course, anyone close to her would die. She wasn't worthy of stable, loving relationships.

Now that she had uncovered these confusing memories of abuse, she absolutely wanted to retreat from the world. She thought she must be tainted, contaminated, and therefore everything she touched would turn to filth. Her family's accusations of her memories being false continuously bounced around her head, and she vowed she would stay locked in the castle until the day she died.

Some days she considered doing everyone a favour and ending it all. The shame was eating her alive, and she wanted it to all be over.

She managed to push away offers of love by locking herself behind the thick defensive castle walls, but she couldn't lock me away. I was with her all along. On the lonely, dark nights, I would remind her that I was still here. I pulled at the thread, which made her heart ache and reminded her that there was a better life waiting for her. She just had to trust me.

The Castle

The duality of the castle,
has suddenly hit home.
As I sit in this turret,
feeling all alone.

This desire to live,
behind walls so strong.
I thought was my saviour,
all along.

Yet the rooms are so shadowy,
so empty and cold.
The chill in the air,
feels stagnant and old.

The castle designed,
to defend and protect.
Has isolated me,
from being able to connect.

I can't help but feel,
so trapped and alone.
An echo of emptiness,
has progressively grown.

Silent tears falling,
Slowly down my face.
Their pain and their heartbreak,
leaving a trace.

What once felt protective,
my safety, my goal.
Is further detaching me,
from the path of my soul.

I feel the deep pull,
from the child within me.
Stoking my fire,
encouraging me to flee.

I cannot stay trapped,
in this castle of mine
I have a quest to complete.
This is my time!

Adult-me lay on the cold, hard floor of the castle she had built up around herself, her body drained from the endless tears; she had nothing left. In that emptiness was a stillness, where she was able to hear a gentle, steady pulse in the distance, calling her forwards, enticing her back onto her path.

She was hearing the whispers to RESTORY her life and to reframe her experiences. Rather than feeling all these bad things happened to her, she was being guided to view them as they were happening for her. They were presenting themselves as gifts that she could learn and grow from. Rather than wallow in self-pity and anguish, she was being urged to question what lessons could be learned. She allowed every one of these life challenges to crack her open, to teach her how to soften. Even though the grief and sadness were overwhelming, every time she experienced one of these heart wrenching traumas, she finally allowed herself to feel all of it.

She was being guided to trust the Universe. She closed her eyes and listened to the messages that were coming into her heart: *Trust that this is all happening for a reason. Trust that this is all part of your transformation. Trust that you are held and supported, and you will rise, stronger than ever before. Remember you are only sent that which you can handle. You've got this. You've come so far. You can't give up now.*

As she softened into the trust, allowing herself to open up, the hard walls of defence began to crack. As each brick began to crumble, she was able to see how far she had already come. From her parent's bitter divorce, she had learned the importance of providing a stable and loving environment for her own family, one that was filled with warmth and honesty and open dialogue. From watching her father become consumed by the evils of alcohol, she learned not to use it to numb out her own pain. From her stepdad's sudden death, she learned not to wait to start living, but to start living her best life now.

Adult-me could see a glimmer of light. She didn't have to be consumed by the heaviness of this trauma. The shocking realisation of childhood abuse was in fact an opportunity for her to grow. She wasn't a bad person. Her abuser was. The shame she had been carrying for decades was not hers to carry. It belonged to her abuser.

As she released these patterns that had been part of her for so long, she began to stand up for herself, trust herself, trust her instinct, trust her body, trust her memories, trust her own truth. She would never go back to living a lie. She had to trust herself, it was the only option. With each breath she took, she told herself it was safe to trust herself. As she did, gradually the castle walls started to crumble. Through the gaps in her defence, she could see a way out, another way of living. She did not need to keep herself locked away, isolated and alone. She had nothing to hide.

Self-doubt tried to pull her back and remind her none of this made sense, but she stood her ground. Her intuition was strong. Whilst she couldn't apply logic and reasoning to these unearthed memories, there was a feeling deep in her gut that knew the truth. Intuition is that immediate feeling you get that appears quicker than your thinking brain can work. We are all born with it. it's our inner compass. When we encounter something that feels good, our whole body expands, becomes open and radiates warmth. If we encounter something that feels wrong however, we can tighten up, shut ourselves down in order to protect ourselves. When we experience pain, we doubt and question ourselves. We withdraw and disconnect from our initial spark of wonder, wholeness and trust.

When it comes to needing answers, we have to root ourselves in our intuition and inner knowing. Remember your inner child is holding the thread that will lead you home. You just have to trust and stop pulling at random threads. Everything you need is already within you. Adult-me had yearned for external validation to tell her she was speaking the truth, but she was slowly awakening to the reality that all she had to do was trust herself. She was finally beginning to soften into that trust and to listen to me and the answers I held.

Some days she could connect easily with me, and other days it was a struggle. To help her in strengthening this bond, she found some old photos of when she was a little girl. She would gaze into the eyes looking back at her in the photographs. The eyes of the five- or six-year-old me had a cheeky mischievous glint, a look of wonder and glee. It was easy to sense that little girl was fully connected to the magic around her.

It was the later photos that kicked her in the gut. In pictures around the age of nine or ten, the face staring back at her at first glance looked perfectly normal, but on second glance, the light in the eyes had clearly been extinguished. The eyes staring back at her in the photograph were blank, empty, vacant. Although there was a smile painted on her face, the eyes no longer shone with feeling. A wave of sadness washed over my adult-self and she felt so much love and protection for the little girl who had the magic ripped out of her. This was when my adult-self really started to feel my presence.

If she closed her eyes and softened into her natural, rhythmical breathing, she could feel into that young version of herself. The part of her that was still very much filled with joy and excitement. She could recall the bubbling sense of enchantment when absorbed in nature. The feeling of happiness when running through the autumn leaves, jumping in puddles, lying in the long grass. The feeling of warmth when the sun shone on her face. The feeling of delight as the rain poured from the sky soaking her skin. The feeling of freedom as the wind whipped up around her, blowing out the cobwebs. When she was in nature, she felt alive, free and happy. This younger version of herself was filled with a fae-like energy that carried an air of mischief and wonder.

As adult-me gazed at the photos she allowed more of the castle walls to tumble down and let the emotions pour out of her. She cried for the child that had her innocence taken away. She cried for the child who was told to be a good girl. She cried for the little girl who believed she was bad. She cried for the little girl who had become so good at wearing a mask.

As each tear fell, they started to wash away the judgement, self-hatred, and fear. As my adult self found herself submerged in the torrent of tears, she realised she was cleansing her past. She was enabling forgiveness and acceptance to rise. The overwhelming sense of compassion for that little girl, for me, was so strong, and I could feel it deeply. I felt heard, seen, accepted and most importantly, loved. I felt completely loved.

At night, adult-me found an old cuddly rabbit that once belonged to her daughter, and she held it tightly. I knew it was her way of holding me, soothing me, reminding me I was safe now, I was supported, I was going to be ok. Those nights were the first time I slept deeply. I felt completely held, nourished, nurtured and loved. It was the most wonderful, warm feeling and one that I will never forget. I had been found. I was safe. I was loved.

Dear Little Katie

When did I let go, of your trembling hand?
When did I banish you, to the forgotten land?
When did I turn my back, and leave you in the cold?
When did I silence, the truth you so deeply hold?
I wish I could turn back time, and caress your little face.
Hold you close to me, in a loving safe embrace.
But I was forced to run away, I simply had to flee.
This overwhelming pain, that was suffocating me.
It was safer to pretend, that you did not exist.
To push down the emotions, to learn to resist.
The sadness you have held, was too overwhelming to feel.
Even though I know, it was the only way to heal.
But I am here now, and I promise I'll never leave.
Healing tears flowing, as I deeply grieve.
You are loved, you are seen, your story will be heard.
I feel your truth, I believe your every word.
For now, we are together, we are stronger as we rise.
With hope and determination, glistening in our eyes.
We are whole, we are complete, and forever bound as one.
No matter what we face, it will be overcome.
United in our pain, of trauma and deep strife.
We set ourselves free, as we RESTORY our life.
Dear Little Katie, thank you for being there
For guiding me back home out of pain and despair.

Behind the tumbling castle walls adult-me reached for my hand. She had finally found a connection back to me and in doing so, I was able to help her further in finding the remaining answers she was looking for. She was still struggling with the big gaps in her memory and she desperately wanted to understand exactly what had happened to her between the ages of seven to eleven. She picked up a pen and asked me to help her remember. She let her pen write.

Do you remember that time at Dad's house? Remember Dad loved to cook, and you used to love sitting and chatting to him whilst he made delicious meals. It was your favourite time with him. Remember he would always have a lager on the go, and he would drink lots as he cooked and chatted. You used to feel really grown up. You liked it when he was still at the lager stage. It was later in the evening when he had the port that it all got a bit scary. Remember he would get angry, fall over and his words would get all slurry. You hated that bit.

Anyway, that particular night, he was still at the lager stage. Do you remember telling him that family member had put cream all over your naked body. You were clearly of an age where it was not appropriate behaviour for an adult male to be rubbing cream over a naked child's body, and Dad got extremely angry. He went mad. And I mean really, really mad. He started shouting and you felt so scared. You were terrified

From that day onwards, you vowed you would never tell anyone ever again. That was the day you finally decided to lock this secret up and pretended it had never happened. Even though you locked it away, it still tried to come out.

Do you remember the nightmares? It was the same one, night after night. You were locked in a room that had no windows or doors. There was no escape. There was a man's voice. You couldn't see the man, but you could hear his words. They would be so loud and booming, taking over all the space in your head. They were nasty, threatening words but you couldn't run away. There was nowhere to go. You hated those dreams. You never understood why you had them at the time, but I knew they scared the life out of you. You hated going to bed because you knew they would be waiting for you. Now I guess you totally understand why they used to come. You didn't want to keep this secret inside of you, and this was your body's way of trying to get this horrid thing out of you..

These two memories were so vivid to adult-me and she remembered them both with such clarity. She knew she had to trust me. She knew I wasn't making this up. Her body knew exactly what had happened to her. Her body remembered everything.

Her inability to enjoy being touched by her loving husband was one example. She never understood why her body would freeze, but now it made sense. She used to be very sexually playful early on in their relationship, but she now realised that she had been using alcohol to assist her. It enabled her to numb out the sensations and play the role of fun, provocative 'Katie'. It was like there were two sides to her. The fun, sexually open, playful version fuelled by alcohol and the scared, anxious version whose entire body would freeze when about to be touched. To the outside world, with alcohol coursing through her bloodstream that 'Katie' was a vivacious, bold character who would often take sexual innuendo too far. Yet, hiding on the inside, was an anxious, confused individual whose body froze with fear of being touched, even being touched by herself.

As each new wave of realisation hit her, the final bricks from the castle walls tumbled down. She had two choices. She could allow herself to be consumed by the falling debris, crushed under their weight, or she could allow the crumbling to crack her open. For so long, she had held everything together so tightly as a means of protecting herself. She had built thick stone walls around her heart. Whilst she thought she was shielding herself from hurt, she was actually preventing love from entering and permeating her being. Her heart had been cracked open with all the pain and sorrow. Her crumbling was going to be the making of her. She was opening up to receiving love.

As she surrendered into trust and allowed the bricks to fall, I watched with great interest. I reassured her that she was going to be ok. She was letting go of control, she was listening, and she was opening up to receiving. She was tapping into her infinite wisdom of her body. She trusted that everything was happening for her and her crumbling was all part of the plan.

As the fallen debris scattered over the forest floor, and the dust settled, she uncovered the next part of the thread: Set boundaries. *Setting clear boundaries is the first step of self-love.* The thing she was about to learn about boundaries is, not everyone will understand them or like them, but that's ok. It's got nothing to do with anyone else. Boundaries are for you to set yourself free.

STEP 5 – ORIENTATE

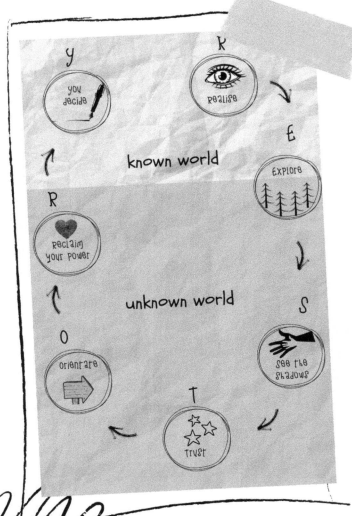

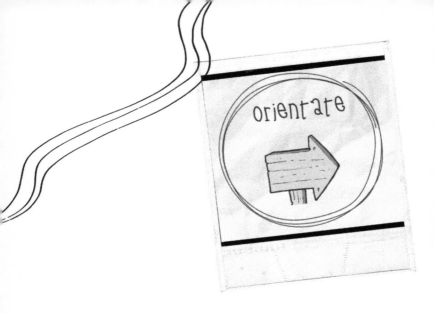

When the hard shell that's held you captive for so long starts to crack, there is space for something new to grow. By letting the protective walls down, you can shine a light on the darkness. The light is able to cascade down, enabling the rich abundant soil to grow new life. You get to decide what the future looks like. It's up to you. Nobody else. Be bold in your choices. Do what you really want to do. If you are unsure what you really want, ask your inner child. They know. They remember what it's like to be alive and filled with curiosity and imagination. Go follow the thread back home. Your inner child will show you the way.

Adult-me wiped the remnants of dust from her eyes and looked around her. The protective castle had fully crumbled, and the fragments of the thick defensive walls were scattered all over the forest floor. As everything settled back into nature's soothing rhythm, she was starting to see life more clearly now. The woods were coming alive in the cold morning air. The freshly spun cobwebs dotted with morning dew were glistening in the early slivers of light. The crisp sun was shining down through the canopy of trees, illuminating a number of possible paths. It was now up to her to decide which path to take.

She was surrounded by a multitude of possibilities. There was one path that would lead her back the way she came, shoving this whole experience back into the box. That path was shrouded in pain, misery, regret, anger and self-hatred. The pain of retracing her steps would be so overbearing and she may not even make it back alive. She knew this was not an option. She had come too far to turn back now.

Another path available to her was to place the mask back on her face and to go on pretending that life was fine. The mask fit so well, as she had worn it for such a long time. She was so accomplished at putting a brave face on, smiling, and performing the role of a happy, content adult. Although she knew if she chose this path, she would have to utilise a number of unhelpful coping strategies to numb out the pain. This path would most likely have led to alcohol to numb the rawness of the pain. She was determined she was not going to follow her father's footsteps. This path was no longer an option.

There was one final path available to her, one that she had never ventured down before. She had no idea what this path would feel like or ultimately where it would lead, but it was the path of openness, honesty, speaking her truth and trusting herself. As she urged herself forwards towards this path, she felt the familiar tug of the thorny branches, desperately trying to hold her back, to keep her locked in a cycle of pleasing others and abandoning herself. But this time her resolve was too strong. This time she was reminded of me, her inner child and the promise she had made me. She had vowed that she would never abandon me again.

Onwards she went, snagging her skin on the thorns, allowing their spikes to draw blood. They couldn't hold her back now. She had a focus that she had never experienced before. She knew that she had to save herself. There was no knight in shining armour about to appear on his horse to whisk her away. This was her time to create her own path. She had to be clear on what she wanted in life. Nothing was going to hold her back.

Occasionally she would hear the familiar cackle of the Wicked Witch, attempting to imprison her once more, trying to convince her that she was worthless and pitiful. But she was determined to keep venturing forwards. She dug deep and remained strong that this was not the truth.

She watched as the dappled sunlight illuminated a path leading her over fallen tree trunks and through moss covered barks. This was unfamiliar territory, but it felt empowering. She decided which way to go, which way to turn. She listened to her heart and took the brave steps towards her new future.

She was beginning to remember what life was like before all the pretending began. She recalled that memory when she was around five years of age, playing in the long grass, feeling the sun on her face. A simpler time when she knew what she wanted, and she wasn't afraid to say it. Here in the midst of nature's beauty, she was reminded of this magic. She felt alive, happy, optimistic, full of imagination and creation.

She was realising her true self had been there all along. It had been hidden under the heaviness of self-hatred and shame. She had previously abandoned herself as a means of survival, but now she was discovering that she could rise up and become whoever she wanted to be. She wasn't stuck. She was being freed from the existence that had held her captive for so long. All that pretence was being been stripped away. Everything that once seemed so solid, so permanent, had in fact crumbled and shattered. In its wake was the rebirth of something beautiful, authentic, honest and true.

As she heard her strong, decisive footsteps hit the forest floor, she made herself some promises. Firstly, she vowed she would no longer say, 'I'm fine.' She had spent too many years pretending, when in fact she was far from fine. She decided that she would always honestly express how she was feeling. No more pretending. No more hiding her truth.

Secondly, she promised me that she would always make me, her inner child, a priority from this day forward. Rather than thinking about what other people wanted, she would ask me what I wanted and really listen to what I had to say. She would no longer agree to go along with things for fear of upsetting others. She would shine her light and allow those who support her in her full luminosity to gravitate towards her.

Thirdly, she agreed that she would ask for help. She had realised there are no medals for being a martyr and struggling alone. For so many years, my adult-self had been fiercely independent and saw it as a strength. The truth was, it was in fact a wound, fuelled by fear. My adult-self believed that she had to do life on her own and never ask for help. Asking for help was letting someone in, being intimate and vulnerable. She didn't feel worthy of inviting someone in to help her. But when she thought of the scared, innocent child within her, then she felt able to ask for help, to let herself be nourished and looked after.

Next, she clarified what her core values were. Our values are our inner-most truth, our spark deep within us. They are often attached to our childlike innocence. My adult self's core values were creativity, excitement, nature and spirituality. This is exactly how I felt when I was playing in the long grass, creating my own magical kingdoms with the insects and the flowers. This was the part of me that had been forgotten, when all the masks and pretending got in the way. I remembered these core values. They were absolutely a part of me. But they just got lost amongst the undergrowth, the tangles of worry and prickly thorns of pain and discomfort. But they were always there. They were just waiting to be found and followed back home.

What do I want?

What do I want?
What ignites my fire?
What do I dream of?
My deepest desire?
I have no idea,
I've simply been guessing.
What do I want in life?
I'm unaccustomed to expressing.
What am I made of?
What do I feel?
What is inauthentic?
And what is real?
Life as I knew it,
has been turned upside down.
Am I treading water?
Or about to drown?
So much of my life,
hidden behind a mask.
Veiled from the reality,
of what has been asked.
Pleasing others had been,
my number one goal.
What I thought would make me,
feel complete and whole.

But all the while,
I had been abandoning me.
Ignoring my desires,
silencing my pleas.
Fiercely independent,
letting nobody in.
Hiding my vulnerability,
behind a very thick skin.
Then I start to consider,
what 'little me' needs.
Listen to her wants,
and her subtle pleads.
Reassuring it is safe,
for her to speak out loud.
To hold her head high,
to be confident and proud.
Feeling into my body,
responding with compassion.
Following my heart's desire,
my deepest passion.
No longer settling,
or simply being just fine.
Living inauthentically,
in this body of mine.
I say no when I want to,
and I say it with grace.

No longer painting a fake smile,
upon my face.
If I am angry, I express it,
I let it run wild.
I release the emotions,
of my inner child.
I follow the light,
that my inner child holds.
As the magic of my soul's path,
tenderly unfolds.
I am my own saviour,
it's up to me to be brave.
There is nobody else,
I am meant to save.

Adult-me knew the journey back home with these new commitments was not going to be an easy one. She would be tempted to revert back to her old ways. She knew she had to put some boundaries in place. Adult-me had very few boundaries. She had been a people-pleaser for so long. It was her survival strategy, and it had become so well-practised that setting limits felt frightening and at times seemed impossible.

For years, she had yearned for approval and love and desperately wanted to avoid any possibility of abandonment. This is why she used to say yes to people. She thought saying yes to people was what she was supposed to do; that's what made her a good girl. The problem with people-pleasing was that adult-me often felt responsible for other people's happiness. She felt like she was somehow responsible for their stories, too.

By not setting boundaries, adult-me had been sacrificing her own values and worth. She was slowly discovering she was not a bad person, and she was starting to realise that boundaries were essential to her happiness. Without boundaries, resentment was able to breed and fester. This was where the hard work had to begin. Adult-me was learning to say no to whatever didn't feel right. Trusting when she was out of alignment with her true self.

It wasn't easy. She had numbed herself for so long that she didn't always know what she wanted. Gradually she started to ask me what I wanted. I got to say what felt right and what didn't. As time went on, this became a routine, and soon her day was filled with all the things she wanted to do. She would see the people she wanted to see and wouldn't waste any more time on things or people that drained her energy. She was aware that she was in control of how she spent her energy. She would gravitate to energy enhancers and avoid the energy vampires.

Setting boundaries was freeing adult-me to be herself.

She was realising that her self-worth was not based on how other saw her. She could not control how others viewed her. Every person she interacted with had their own version of a story about her and who she was. That had nothing to do with her. The only story she had to focus on was the one she was telling herself. By practising self-acceptance, she was discovering she did not need to give anyone else the power of affirming her worth.

The biggest test came when she viewed her relationship with her own family in Wales. Whilst she was longing for them to believe her, she knew she could not control this situation. They had their own stories to unravel, and that was not anything to do with adult-me. Adult-me had to learn to step out of the way, even though it pained her so much. She desperately wanted to show them her truth, but she knew they wouldn't and couldn't see it. Adult-me made the heart-breaking decision to continue venturing forwards on her own path without these people in her life. She had come too far now to be told that she had made this all up. She had self-belief coursing through her veins, and it was such an empowering feeling she was not going to stop it now. She trusted her own body. She trusted her memories. She trusted her intuition, and that was enough. If certain family members were not able to believe her, then that was their choice. Adult-me explained to them that until they were prepared to join her on this journey into discovering the truth, she could no longer have them in her life. If one day they felt able to explore this part of the forest, then adult-me promised she would be there to help guide the way. But until that day, she was going forwards on her own. She valued her life too much to be held back.

The wonderful thing with self-worth is that once you start to accept you are worthy of great things, you will start to attract great things. Adult-me had tried doing this the wrong way round for so long. She thought she had to prove to others that she was worthy of great things. She was actually in control of how she saw herself, nobody else.

She had been trapped in a cycle of caring what others thought of her. She tried so hard to get external validation, but it was beyond her control. It was an impossible task. As soon as she discovered this, she set herself free. She was stepping out of her old comfort zone and starting to fall in love with the person she was, the person she had always been.

As this great awareness settled, the path before her opened up into the most beautiful, expansive clearing. The tangled branches were a distant memory and a great vastness of space appeared before her. The trees formed a wide, open circle, holding space for adult-me to step forward. The leaves created a soft carpet, cushioning her feet. The sun poured down, allowing new growth to sprout on the forest floor. This clearing felt abundant, full of hope and optimism. Adult-me felt free and her heart leapt with joy. The heavy density of the forest had lifted. She was aligning with her values of excitement, creativity, nature and spirituality. She didn't need anyone or anything externally to validate her worth.

For the first time ever, she was holding my hand and asking me what I wanted. She protected me with clear boundaries and said no to anything that dimmed my light. She was allowing me, her inner child, to be seen and heard, and it felt so good. I liked where this path was leading. It felt like we were going home.

Here in the middle of the clearing of the forest, with the sunlight pouring down, she uncovered the next part of the thread: *Love and accept all of you.* She was being guided to realise in the aftermath of trauma, it was essential to relocate all the lost parts of her fragmented self and love and nurture each and every one of them. They were all welcome. They were all essential to her healing.

STEP 6 –
RECLAIM YOUR POWER

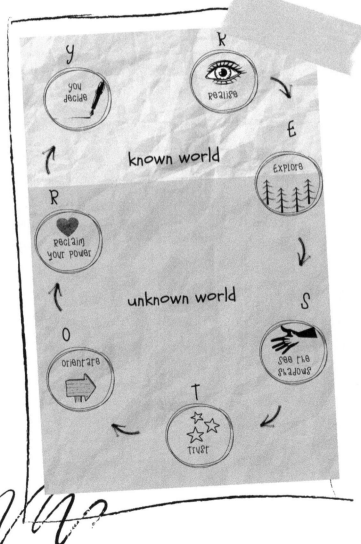

known world

- Y — you decide
- R — realise
- E — explore

unknown world

- R — reclaim your power
- O — orientate
- S — see the shadows
- T — trust

Gather together all the fragmented parts of you that got lost along the way. Pick them up, dust them off, hold them, love them and nurture them. They are all part of you. There are no bad bits and good bits. They are what makes you whole. Love them for what they are, for what they have been through. Piece yourself back together again. Reclaim your power. Release your wings and fly higher than you have ever flown before. You are incredible. You deserve the best in life. Go fly!

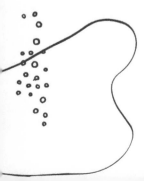

Adult-me started walking forwards with a determination and clarity she had never felt before. Even though there was no clear path, she was courageously constructing her own. She was no longer following someone else's footsteps, nor was she allowing herself to be enticed back down her well-trodden path of self-limiting beliefs and thought patterns. This path was untouched, and it was hers. To support her in ensuring this pathway was clear and free from entanglement, she had to reconnect with all the parts of herself that she had turned her back on, buried in shame and regret.

Adult-me was taking decisive steps towards her future life, armed with the knowledge that she was worthy. With this inner strength, she was able to accept all past mistakes and forgive herself. There were parts of her fragmented soul that still needed to be located. They were still a part of her. She couldn't neglect them, or pretend they weren't there. All parts of her story were valid and worthy. It was time to face them and reclaim them.

Firstly, she made peace with her memory loss. She used to feel that there was something wrong with her because she couldn't recall a large part of her childhood. She had no memory of her junior school, which she attended from the ages of eight to eleven years. She couldn't understand why she had no recollection of her childhood bedroom. When old friends reminisced about their adventures together, there was nothing, no memory, just a black hole of nothingness. For so many years, my adult-self blamed herself for this and assumed there was something wrong with her, that she was somehow broken. Yet, she was understanding the link between memory loss and trauma and was starting to accept that it was quite normal to have blocks of memory loss when in a high state of anxiety. This survival technique might have wiped out large chunks of her childhood, but it also kept her protected from them. Now they had started to resurface, she was able to be gentle with herself and her memory loss. She was not broken. She allowed her memory loss to become a part of who she was. It had served its purpose of protecting her and for that she was truly grateful.

The next step she had to accept was her behaviour in her teenage years. Thinking back to this time filled her with so much embarrassment and shame. She had been an extreme risk taker. She was drinking excessively, taking drugs and being very sexually promiscuous. In the peak of her drug-taking, she was consuming multiple ecstasy tablets and speed in a night. The worst part of her drug-fuelled existence was when she was around 17 years of age and she spontaneously booked a flight departing the following day to Ibiza. She was the only female on this trip. She spent a week with seven males, taking excessive amounts of drugs every single day. She was lucky to have survived. Adult-me can now completely understand why it was so desirable to 'get off her head' for prolonged periods of time. She was desperately trying to get away from these hateful memories that were eating her up inside. Her excessive drinking would lead to one-night stands which at times put her in very dangerous situations. It wasn't unusual for her to be walking the streets on her way home, in the early hours of the morning, having been kicked out of some one-night stand's house once she was surplus to requirements. This period of her life had been incredibly lonely and painful. She was discovering that this sort of behaviour was not unusual among childhood sexual abuse survivors. Periods of sexual promiscuity and poor self-esteem can be common reactions to childhood sexual abuse. Substance abuse is also another frequent signal of abuse. It is not uncommon for people to become addicted to alcohol or drugs, and to take them in excess. As adult-me was discovering these facts, she was able to understand why her behaviour throughout her teenage years had been so destructive. The missing pieces were slotting into place. Now, as my adult-self reflected back on this period of her life, she was beginning to feel love and compassion for this adolescent that was clearly deeply struggling and feeling all alone. She accepted these parts of herself and could see that they were simply a massive cry for help.

She was also coming to terms with her difficulties with intimacy. Despite being married for 15 years to a wonderfully supportive husband, she found intimacy extremely uncomfortable. In the early days in her relationship, sex was very playful, when she was able to play a role of being a sexual and seductive partner but as the relationship proceeded and deepened, she started to shut down sexually. The reality of being tenderly caressed, made her whole body freeze. There were also certain intimate acts that she point-blank refused. She once again assumed there was something wrong with her and that she was somehow broken. Now she was understanding how common this was for people who had been abused. Yet another jigsaw piece slotted into place.

Anger was rising to the surface. She was furious that this hidden trauma had permeated into so many aspects of her life. It took away years of her childhood memory; it propelled her into alcohol, drugs and sexual promiscuity in her teenage years. It had also robbed her of years of intimacy with her husband. She was feeling intense anger that it had affected so many parts of her existence. She was also angry that people had their suspicions about this family member but pretended it wasn't happening. She was angry that she was being blamed for speaking up. She was angry that she wasn't believed. She had to allow herself to feel this anger and allow it be part of her. To try and heal without accepting the anger was futile. She couldn't just jump to compassion and forgiveness. That wouldn't work. She had to feel it all.

By allowing herself to feel anger towards her abuser, to all the people who hid it, to all the people who continued to deny it happened, to the FMSF for all the damage they had done, she was enabling herself to heal. By letting all this rage out of her, she was equally allowing herself to soften and forgive herself. Adult-me was being called to forgive herself for all the times she turned her back on herself, for when she abandoned herself to try to please others. For when she wore a brave face and lied about the pain that she was really feeling. For all the horrible things she said to herself, for all the drugs and alcohol she inflicted on herself. For all the one-night stands and self-abuse she opted for. Now she could see it through the eyes of compassion and she totally understood why she acted in this way. The self-hatred and shame were now able to melt away.

Shame is such a heavy emotion. It keeps us stuck in old patterns. Adult-me had come too far to allow shame to drag her backwards. Shame tries to wrap its tendrils around us in an attempt to drag us back into the familiar patterns of self-loathing and disgust, and it's all too easy to allow ourselves to get sucked back into that downward spiral. It's an automatic response. We have done it for so many years. We could even do it with our eyes closed.

My adult self was learning to accept that even though she had been shattered by her past experiences, all the fragments of her pain and suffering were essential to her feeling whole. This was the phase where the brave face had to ripped off and all the raw, honest truth shown to the world. Adult-me was allowing the angry, resentful, bitter, wounded, shameful sides of her to be seen. They were being uncovered and laid bare for all to see. They were all part of her, and now it was time to accept them all. This was the moment to look at her face in the mirror and fully accept and love what she saw.

The Mirror

As I glance into the mirror,
at my honest reflection.
I linger on my face,
the quality of my complexion.
Scrutinising every blemish,
That's been etched onto my face.
Every line can tell a story,
their pain has left a trace.
The mirror is a portal,
into my deepest truth.
It's been the great reflector,
since the beginning of my youth.
Watching as I navigate,
through the waves of my healing.
The seer into my heart,
projecting what I'm feeling.
Relinquishing the mask,
shown to the world outside.
There is no need to pretend,
no longer will I hide.
The truth behind the brave face,
is one that feels intensely.
Sadness, grief and anger,
pouring out immensely.
My mirror holds my gaze,
as shame exits my pores.

Acknowledging the pain,
of the internal wars.
All parts of me are welcome,
all parts of me laid bare.
Casting light upon my anguish,
acknowledging my despair.
The fragments of my soul,
that were lost over the years.
Reclaimed and washed clean,
with my aching tears.
No part of me deemed bad,
no part of me rejected.
Welcoming back the parts of me,
I have so often neglected.
The light pours on my reflection,
illuminating my soul.
Piecing me back together,
making me feel whole.
Loving every part of me,
forgiving the mistakes I made.
Soothing my inner child,
who's scared and afraid.

I gaze into my eyes,
And connect to my inner fire.
I am ready to step forward,
with passion and desire.
I have what it takes,
I have already survived so much.
I will bounce back,
Future–me is within touch.
I shall reclaim my power,
and from the ashes I will rise.
I'll wipe the tears of heartache,
from my reddened eyes.
There are no more secrets hiding,
in the corners of my soul.
The mirror knows the truth,
I am complete and I am whole.

My adult self was coming to terms with all parts of herself. The ones in plain sight and the parts that were hidden inside. To the outside world, adult-me was organised, calm, loving, helpful and efficient. What the outside world didn't realise was the existence of the parts that remained hidden from view. The ashamed part of her was proving to be the hardest to let go of. This was the part that was there in the background, constantly picking at the scabs as soon as they started to heal. This part had one goal and that was to inflict as much pain as possible. The shame part had no off switch. Behind closed doors, the ashamed part would leak out of the cracks and engulf adult-me in a tsunami of self-hatred. It was always threatening to pour out.

Adult-me realised the time had come to let all the shame out. Let it show itself to the world. Tell others that it existed. As she continued venturing forwards through the forest, crushing any obstacles in her way, pushing aside the brambles and nettles, she allowed the shame to seep out of her body. Surrounded by nature's sacred embrace, she was invited to let it out for once and for all. In the midst of the trees, she let the shame leach out of her being, her wail reverberating off the ancient oaks. This was not hers to carry. She allowed it to pour out of her, knowing that it would be transmuted by the healing properties of the forest. With each purge of shame, she was creating more and more space inside of her. As the waves of self-hatred, guilt, and self-loathing flowed out of her, she was reclaiming her power.

She was really beginning to trust her intuition and continued to follow the thread. She was so close now. She allowed the parts of her that had been locked up, held back, and hidden to come to the surface. I was coming to the surface. As my adult-self opened herself up to the faith and optimism I held, the path ahead of her became clearer. What once was tangled branches of confusion and constant dead ends was now a hopeful pathway through the trees. With each brave footstep towards loving and accepting her whole self, the pathway became clearer, freer of debris. The trees had formed an arched pathway, the leaves created soft cushioning, the sunlight dappled the ground. My adult-self was reclaiming her power and it felt good. I took hold of her hand and led her through the archway.

Adult-me had spent so many years looking outside of herself, dreaming for a better version, thinking that this version was somehow broken and not enough. But as soon as she started to look inside, she awakened to the truth that she was whole, she was complete. Her wounds had started to heal, and yes, they were leaving scars, but those scars were a constant reminder that she had fought battles and won. They were nothing to be ashamed of. Quite the opposite. They were memories of the trauma and a reminder that she had overcome so much. They were her medals in her hero's journey.

As adult-me held my hand, she felt the final part of the thread: *Transmute the pain into power. Use the suffering as fuel for your growth. You are transforming into greatness.*

STEP 7 – YOU DECIDE

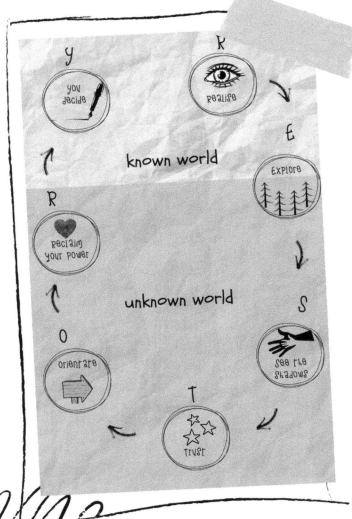

Listen to the whispers and follow the thread back home. Follow your inner child. They will lead you to the light within. It has been there all along. It just got hidden amongst the shadows and the tangled thorns.

As the realisation dawns that nobody is coming to save you, you rise as the hero in your own journey. You decide how your story unfolds.

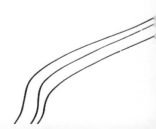

Adult-me walked through the arched pathway, noticing how vivid everything seemed. The sounds, smells and sights of the forest all seemed to be alive and bubbling with new possibilities. She turned, glanced back and realised how far she had come.

She took a moment to reflect on the progress she had made on this journey. When she first embarked on this adventure, she didn't even know I existed. She was living her life behind a mask and constantly searching externally for true happiness. She would pull at random threads, hoping they would bring her fulfilment, but they never did. She was living her life in a deep amnesic sleep. She found the concept of self-love bewildering. Even though she was teaching it to thousands of children, she felt unable to embrace it herself. She did not feel like she was worthy of it. She felt like she was bad, rotten to the core.

As adult-me had previously refused the call to adventure a number of times, it finally came back with such force that she had no option but to accept it. As the horrors of her realisation that she had been sexually abused as a child emerged, she was catapulted into the depths of the forest. It was dark and scary. There were unfamiliar noises and shadows that followed her. She hit dead ends, got tangled in the thorny branches and found herself caught in the Wicked Witch's cage. Here she surrendered to the spiteful words. By allowing these dark, hidden aspects to revel themselves, they started to lose their potency, and adult-me was able to see her truth. It was here that she discovered me.

With my hand in hers, she attempted to forge her path onwards, but the fears of self-doubt were all-consuming. She locked herself away behind the thick walls of the castle to protect herself from feeling. She wanted everything to just go away. But that was not possible. Adult-me was not going to allow herself to shatter into a million pieces and remain broken. She was destined to bounce back. With the crumbling of the castle walls, she felt the beginnings of something new. A feeling inside of her that urged her to trust herself, to follow her intuition, to listen to her body. She was listening to the messages her body held. She pushed aside the anguish of self-doubt and trusted me, her inner child. After all, I was the only one who was there.

There was a source of power within her that was gathering momentum. It was guiding her onwards, through the trees and she found herself in a clearing. From this expansive space she was able to view the multitude of pathways available to her. Some looked familiar, old patterns of self-limiting beliefs, old narratives calling out to her. She could easily have followed one of these, slipping back into an unfulfilled existence. Yet, she chose to keep forging her own path. This one had not been ventured down before. This new pathway was one that aligned with who she was destined to be. She had clarity of her values, her boundaries and her innermost desires. She had made a promise to honour her own needs and to no longer people-please. She knew she had to leave behind the people who did not align with her future. She did this with loving kindness and ventured onwards. She kept going when the branches caught her footing; she continued putting one foot in front of the other, with a hope and determination in her eyes that refused to falter.

As she forged this new pathway through the forest, she gathered together all the fragmented parts of her soul that had been lost over the years. She lovingly pieced them back together. They were not parts of her past that were to be discarded. They were an essential part of her healing. By embracing her imperfections and flaws and wearing her scars with pride, she was rising, with such strength and determination. She was reminded of the Japanese art of kintsugi of putting broken pottery pieces back together with gold. As she was embracing her flaws and imperfections, and piecing herself back together again, she was creating an even stronger, more beautiful version of herself.

Adult-me reached inside her soul and once more took hold of my hand. She wrapped her fingers around mine and felt the end of the golden thread. She read the final message one more time. *Transmute the pain into power. Use the suffering as fuel for your growth. You are transforming into greatness.* She knew this could mean only one thing. There was one final task for her to complete before she was able to fully embrace the reward. The reward was the thing that she had been searching for her whole life. It was the answer to her prayers. It was the elusive key to unlocking true happiness.

As the reward was so precious, it had been guarded by a magnificent fire-breathing dragon. Dragons have been feared by many, largely owing to our story books depicting these mighty creatures as destructive and vicious. I, however, knew that dragons were immense healers. They can burn away pain, and from the ashes they enable a stronger version of you to rise. Dragons teach us that we have the power to transmute all our pain into healing. We can grow, evolve and rise, stronger than before. Dragons have been guardians of these ancient truths and protectors of the great reward. The time had come for adult-me to embrace the healing energy of the dragon collective and uncover the final reward.

Dragons

I felt the deep intensity of pain,
Piercing my heart again and again.
Ragged shards of shame discarded on the path,
Waves of despair in the aftermath.

A deep remembering from the core of my soul,
That I lost part of me, my right to be whole.
An innocence stolen, snatched from my grasp,
No matter how hard I tried to clasp.

Wandering lonely, lost and afraid,
Stepping off the path, I courageously strayed.
Each step spewing truths on the ground,
Unearthing their secrets, longing to be found.

The fear of doubt, being called mad,
Being branded insane, rotten and bad.
When in fact what is rising is greater than me,
A fearlessness revealing this atrocity.

At the edge of the forest hidden from the path,
Dormant, yet poised with its pent-up wrath.
Lies the dragon awaiting in its cavernous lair,
Ready to destroy the root of despair.

. Calling upon the energy of that mighty beast,
To ward off the vermin that skulk underneath.
Urging the cracks to expose themselves wide,
Revealing this rancidity held inside.

Calling in energy from the dragon collective,
To heal my body and keep me protected.
Utilising their fire to transmute my pain,
Alchemising it back to pure love again.

Releasing the fear with each breath of fire,
Consenting to the healing as it begins to transpire.
Surrender, trust, lay it out to be burned,
Grateful for the wisdom of the lesson learned.

Drawing in forgiveness, letting go of the grief,
Basking in the transformative light beneath.
Sensing their presence as they circle above,
Transmuting my pain into an everlasting love.

Adult-me allowed all her pain and suffering to be transmuted by the dragon. She could not change her past. It had already happened. But she could allow the experiences to propel her into a world she never knew existed. The dragon's fiery breath scorched the remaining traces of sadness, grief, anger, heartache, resentment, and loss. As it transmuted the final shards of pain, she finally saw it. The brilliance of the light almost took her breath away. It was the final reward of her mighty quest. There before her was the most spellbinding, sacred, crystalline gemstone. It's rays of rainbow light bounced all around her. It was completely hypnotising. The ethereal glow instantly filled her with a love so deep. A love for herself and her inner child, for everything they had endured. This overwhelming feeling was the most expansive thing she had ever felt.

Adult-me could barely believe what she was seeing. The light from this incredible, vibrant precious gemstone was coming from her. It wasn't buried in the soil or attached high up on a tree. It wasn't hidden in the dragon's cave or concealed within the Witch's cauldron. It was inside her and it had been all along. She had spent so many years thinking self-love was outside of her, attached to external validation. Yet it was there all along, just buried under her own pain, suffering, self-hatred, fear. Having allowed herself to be cracked open, it gave space for the light within her to shine. It was guiding adult-me back home.

With the gemstone radiating love and light from her inner being, adult-me couldn't wait to share this gift with the world. The dragon's work was done and as it turned and took flight through the canopy of trees, adult-me caught a glimpse of her ordinary world. She found that she was running towards the edge of the forest, eager to share this wisdom with others.

Normally, when I come to the end of a story in one of

my fairy tale books, when we reach the conclusion of the magnificent quest, when the hero makes their way back home, there is a grand finale, the unveiling of the 'Happily Ever After'. The kingdom erupts in a joyous celebration filled with excitement and delight. There are feasts and dancing. The birds sing and the sun shines.

As adult-me emerged out of the forest and stepped back into her ordinary world, there were no fanfares, no invitations to Royal Balls, no lavish parades in the street. People didn't break out in joyous song, celebrating their hero was home. Life looked very similar to how it did when she left on this journey. There were, however, a number of key differences from the world she left, all that time ago. The most pertinent one was she had found me. There was a childlike joy in her that was eager to be seen, a fae-like energy that wanted to play and have fun. She was so grateful to have this part of her reconnected. It helped her when she thought about the gaping hole of her absent family members in Wales. When she embarked on this journey, before she found the courage to speak her truth, they were still part of her life. Now they were not. However, she had learned this painful absence was a necessary part of her growth. It was all part of her bounce back. The only way she could continue to have these people in her life was to go back to living a lie. To pretending that she had made it up and to apologise for the inconvenience she had caused. Maybe the previous version of adult-me would have done that. She would have attempted to clean up her mess and shove all the shame back down into the box.

But to do this would mean she would have to abandon me, her inner child, once more. She had been given a life-changing decision. She could choose to neglect herself to please others and continue living a lie. Or she could stand in her power, own her truth, and unapologetically lay her soul bare for all to see. She had nothing to hide. There were no more secrets within her. Powered by the magnificent gemstone, she chose to shine her light, to guide her forwards on the path of self-love and self-respect.

You may wonder if now that she was in possession of this beautiful gemstone, that meant she no longer felt any pain or suffering, and every day was filled with love and light. Sadly not. That might very well be the case in the fairy tales, but in the real world it is impossible to feel happy all of the time. In the real world there were days when adult-me felt as if she had lost the guiding light, and she stumbled backwards, catching her scars in the thorny branches once again.

Her old coping mechanisms were not completely eradicated. They still came back from time to time. It was such a familiar way for her body to feel. The Witch would rise up every now and then and try to convince her she was worthless. Some days, adult-me was able to see it was just the old woman imparting her wisdom and lessons. Other days, she would forget and once more feel trapped and alone. This is all part of the healing journey. Remember, at the very beginning I explained it is not a straight line from A to B. It looks more like this.

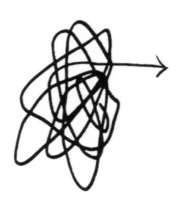

I think so many people assume it is just a hop, skip and jump to reach a life free of pain, but that isn't the case. The sooner we all accept that life is like a tangled, messy pathway, the easier it is. This false hope that if we reach spiritual enlightenment then life will be absolutely perfect, is just the stuff of make believe. The magic exists in how we choose to navigate our way on this messy path.

Adult-me was in possession of this magic and she showed us that it is ok to take small steps, sometimes forwards, sometimes backwards, and sometimes sideways. The magic happened every time she caught herself being pulled backwards, repeating the old patterns. Whenever this happened, she noticed it, and she was able to pull out the thorns before they pierced her skin. She had accepted that the thorns will still be there, but she had a choice as to whether they got stuck and ripped open her scars or simply snagged her clothing as a reminder of her past.

Future-me

When I gaze into the future,
What do I see?
Who is this,
Future version of me?
What does she look like?
What clothes does she wear?
Where does she live?
What colour's her hair?
The picture may lack clarity,
Yet one thing is clear
Inside future—me,
There's a distinct lack of fear.
There are no more secrets,
Burning a hole inside.
No shame, no guilt,
No need to hide.
Future—me can comfortably,
Gaze into her eyes.
No need to stifle,
Her tormented cries.
No more pretending,
No mask to wear.
No heavy layer of shame,
With its burden to bear.
She's free to express,
To be seen and be heard.

Sharing her poetry,
The ache of each word.
Voicing her emotions,
Through her sketches and prose.
Without worrying if anyone,
Likes how it goes.
Future—me steps up,
Takes hold of my hand.
Leading me onwards,
From the forgotten land.
I feel safe, I feel loved,
I feel calm and at ease.
As we navigate our way,
Through the labyrinth of trees.
Future—me is not,
Some dramatic unveiling.
Wiping out my mistakes,
Erasing each failing.
Creating a sparklier,
Version of me.
All polished and primed,
for the world to see.
Future—me bares bruises,
And carries the scars.
Reflected under the light,
Of the moon and the stars.

She accepts herself wholly,
With nothing to hide.
Her inner child standing,
Right by her side.
It might not look pretty,
All tidy and neat.
But it's real,
With its own pulsing heartbeat.
Raw, uncensored,
Honest, and free.
This is the version,
Of future-me.

Adult-me felt the source of light emanating from the gemstone within her. It enabled her to connect to a greater power, a deeper sense of spirituality. She surrendered to the Universe and allowed herself to be guided. She filled herself up with yoga, reiki, meditation, oracle cards, manifestation, poetry and art. Adult-me allowed herself to once more feel the connection to nature and elemental energy. This was always a side to her that she hid and felt embarrassed of. She had been worried what people would think of her. Whilst she didn't actually believe there were fairies at the bottom of the garden, she did feel a connection to the playful, fae-like energy that was very present in the woodlands around her home. She felt the magical quality in the air when surrounded by trees, moss, and ferns. She was not afraid to embrace that magical quality. It was authentically her. She had fully opened herself up to the Universe and was allowing her life to unfold, exactly as intended. This made her feel safe, supported, nurtured and held.

When we started this journey adult-me was living her life behind a mask, desperately trying to please others, seeking external validation to fill a void that she had become so accustomed to. Her life seemed full on the surface but deep down, adult-me was just full of self-loathing. Her RESTORY journey through the woods enabled her to release all this rancidity she held inside and to purge all the shadows that had dimmed her light. She realised she was now in control of the pen and she had a story to write.

The blurb on the back of her story book would read:

Katie reconnected with all the lost parts of her soul and pieced each one back together with tenderness and grace. Her inner child was her guiding light, reminding her where to find love, laughter, joy and happiness. Katie shone her light so authentically and brightly that others were inspired to forge their own path through the woods. Katie showed us that with courage it is always possible to transmute pain into light and create our own 'Happily Ever After'.

RESTORY - THE END

Sharing my RESTORY journey with you has been deeply healing. Thank you for taking the time to hear my truth. It has been quite an adventure and one that has taken me to places I never knew existed. I'm not going to pretend that it was an easy journey, but I am so glad I kept going, even on the darkest of days.

I am so grateful to my inner child for not giving up on me when I had so clearly given up on finding her. Reuniting with my eight-year-old self has brought so much joy, love, gratitude and compassion. I always found the concept of self-love mind boggling. Yet, when you face your own inner child who is feeling scared, lost, afraid and wounded, it is impossible not to love this part of you. The tears poured from my eyes as I held my inner child, soothed her, told her she was safe and reassured her she was not a bad girl. How could I not love this child? How could I not love this part of me?

Once I allowed my heart to crack open and embrace this side of me, the rest just followed. I surrendered to her and allowed her to lead me. She seemed to know exactly where to go. I had forgotten what a feisty, brave, wild child she was, deeply connected to nature and happiest when her face was smeared with mud and grass in her hair.

There were days when the pain was all-consuming, and I didn't want to continue on this journey, but she would tug at the thread and remind me that a life I was yearning for was waiting for me. I just had to follow the thread back home. So I did. Time and time again, I picked myself up off the forest floor, dusted myself down and continued taking the baby steps.

What I learned along the way was every time I told myself I wasn't good enough, or I doubted myself, I was once again rejecting that little girl. Hasn't she been through enough? Why would I continue to doubt this innocent, gentle, pure child? For some reason it is easy for us to be unkind and harsh to our adult selves, but start to see it through the eyes of your inner child. How does that constant criticism and judgement make them feel? I had to learn to celebrate all the small wins, no matter how insignificant they seemed; they all mattered. Every time I gave myself a pat on the back, it was a huge gesture of encouragement to my inner child. She felt seen and loved.

On the really dark days, I would struggle to do anything. I allowed myself the time and space to stop. I stopped my business, which in turn stopped my busy-ness. In this stillness, I allowed the emotions to rise. Some days, they were overwhelming, and I would release an animalistic wail. Other days, the sobs would be silent but heart-wrenching. The most important thing was letting them out. Letting the tears flow. They had been held in for so long, and their release was so cathartic.

Once I moved past the raw stages of grief, I would fluctuate between ok days and bad days. On the bad days I just wanted to be alone, to feel the force of the emotions. Some days, I felt stuck, frozen in the intensity of the emotions and couldn't seem to pull myself out of the pit. The feelings of shame and self-hatred would stick to me like a noxious tar, as emotional energy was getting stored in my muscles and tissues. I was experiencing chronic neck and shoulder pain and extremely debilitating headaches.

To ease the physical discomfort, I tried a range of body work modalities including Body Stress Release, reflexology, reiki and massage. These all gradually helped to shift this trapped emotion that had burrowed its way deep into my being. I practised gentle yoga to allow the prana to once more flow through my body.

When I was feeling stuck, I would force myself to go for a walk to help shift the stagnation. Being outside had an incredible impact on my state of mind. I somehow managed to move the heaviness a little, jolt it into moving. Shame hangs over us in a heavy way, and the simple act of getting the heart pumping and moving my limbs somehow managed to get it to shift. So, if you are going through your own RESTORY journey and you too feel stuck and unable to move on, go outside for a walk and just see if you can feel that subtle shift into realising that life will get better.

When I felt I was going round in circles, I would check in to see whether or not I was living my life in alignment with my values. Checking in with the areas that felt honest and authentically me was a daily reminder of when I was out of balance. My values are creativity, excitement, nature and spirituality, so every day I would try to ensure I did one thing that brought me back into balance. I could be as simple as making a warm, nourishing cacao and drinking it whilst playing with my favourite oracle card deck. It could be doing something utterly spontaneous and childlike, or it could simply be writing a poem. When these aspects were not in my life, life felt flat.

The one thing that always improved my mood was being in nature. It is one of my values and it is deeply healing. Allowing the elements to work their magic on you – whether it's feeling the force of the wind blowing out the cobwebs, the rain washing away your pain, or the sun filling you with light – is so invigorating. Also, spend time in the environment that you feel most deeply connected to, whether it is the ocean, mountains, rivers or woods. I promise you that you will absolutely feel more like yourself when you are surrounded by this elemental energy.

Another method I used to help shift me forwards was inviting my inner child out to play. Writing this book showed me that my inner child can teach me so much about how to be happy. We are so very serious as adults, and we forget to play. This doesn't mean picking up dolls and having a tea party, unless that does light you up, of course, in which case, go for it. Your playtime is totally unique to you. For me it was watching Disney films such as Maleficent and Into the Woods, baking cakes, drawing dragons and making model fairies out of wire. It is totally up to you what you do; ask your inner child what they would like to do today.

Finally, I would use meditation to help me get out of a stagnant state. As one of my values is excitement, I struggle with doing the same daily practice. I need to shake it up. Some days I would meditate sitting up, others lying down, sometimes I would listen to a guided mediation, and others I would repeat a mantra. How I meditated wasn't important, but what was important was carving out some time to connect to my higher self, to the Universe and to listen. There are so many insights available to us if we just listen. It can be as simple as just closing your eyes for five minutes and listening to what arises.

I summarised these steps into the acronym MAGIC to remind me that it was possible to get myself out of a state of stagnation and to move through the seven RESTORY steps. If we are willing to open ourselves up, we will see there is always magic around. If you would like to delve deeper into the MAGIC please visit www.andthenkatie. com where I have shared the practises that supported me on my journey.

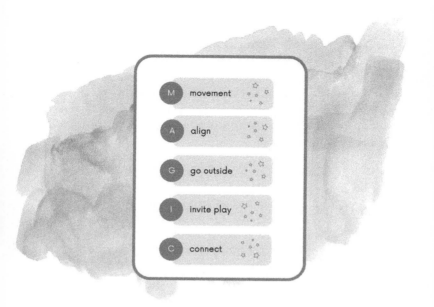

By applying MAGIC to my days, I was able to see that the gemstone was still there. It is always there. We just lose sight of it. We focus on searching externally, when all along that which we seek is inside of us.

My daily practice now revolves around the gemstone. If I feel off balance or out of alignment, I work through the seven RESTORY stages which enables me to dust off the gemstone and allow its guiding light to shine once more. This ensures I stay on the path to fulfilling my purpose. If I get lost, I use the thread to lead me back to the seven key messages: *Listen to the niggle; Step into the unknown; Make friends with your shadow side; Follow your intuition; Set boundaries; Accept all parts of you; Transmute all pain into power.*

So, how does it feel to be back home? Is life massively different? Is every day now filled with pure love and light? Well, the honest answer is no. I think this is one of the great illusions of the self-help industry. We are led to believe that there is a world waiting for us that is so vastly different from the life we currently have. This new version of ourselves is like a total overhaul of who we are today. We set ourselves completely unrealistic expectations and this only leads us to feeling inadequate, disappointed and lacking.

What my journey has taught me is that my life is enough, as it is. In my search for a better version of me, I had abandoned and discarded myself as not being good enough. I was searching for a shinier, newer, upgraded version of me. But I realised that there is nothing wrong with this version. I am enough. I have always been enough. In my search externally, I had missed what was here all along. It wasn't outside of me. It was within me all this time.

Perhaps this is where we turn to Maureen Murdock's version of the Hero's Journey called The Heroine's Journey: Woman's Quest for Wholeness. Murdock, a student of Joseph Campbell, developed the original male-centric monomyth to focus specifically on women's spiritual journeys, which had previously been disregarded by Campbell. He had stated in 1981 *'Women don't need to make the journey. In the whole mythological tradition, the woman is there. All she has to do is to realise that she's the place that people are trying to get to'* (Campbell, 1981).

Murdock's version, The Heroine's Journey sees the female protagonist turn inward to reclaim the power and spirit of her sacred feminine. In the final stages of her journey, she remembers her true nature and accepts herself as she is, integrating both the masculine and feminine. It is a moment where the Heroine recognises her wounds, thanks them for all they have taught her and then she lets them go. This is clearly represented in the final stages of the RESTORY journey where I learned to reclaim all the lost fragments of myself and piece them back together with tenderness and grace. What followed was the delicate art of integrating the feminine and masculine aspects of my being.

Having ripped of the mask, I now allow more vulnerability to show. Life is lighter, freer, more honest, raw, authentic and true. I no longer abandon myself in pursuit of pleasing others, I no longer ignore my inner child and what she wants. I am aware when my wounded child reacts, and I am now equipped to reparent her and soothe her, so she doesn't feel the need to take over. I am clear on my values and my desires. I check in every day with what feels good to me, and then I do that. I share my truth, and I am completely honest with myself. I no longer pretend I'm ok when I'm not, and I hopefully inspire others to do the same. I allow my bare soul to be seen without fear. There is magic in my life now, and I allow myself the time to see it and appreciate it. I feel safe to trust myself and I allow love to permeate every cell of my body. I pause every day to feel grateful for my journey.

I was once trapped in a world of self-hatred, shame, and fear, and was constantly running away from these parts of me. Yet, the minute I stopped and allowed them all to be seen, I realised they were not the terrifying monsters I thought they were but in fact they were the honest and raw parts of me. By facing these parts of me I have been able to fall in love with who I've always been.

I would love to invite you to come onto this journey. You must come exactly as you are. I want you to feel safe enough that you can open yourself up and allow all the messy contents to spill out onto the floor. There is nothing to be ashamed of. All parts of you are welcome here. You are not broken. Take a deep breath and take the leap into the unknown. This is your story and you get to choose how it unfolds.

The final stage of the Heroine's Journey sees the protagonist integrating the feminine and masculine and then sharing this knowledge to help others also reclaim this balance. This is something that I feel extremely passionate about. Having gone through this deep transformation myself, I now wish to support others in taking their own courageous steps into the forest to face their shadows and heal the wounds. It is worth every single step into the unknown. This next part of the book will support you as you navigate your way through the RESTORY stages.

Remember this is your story. You own it. Nobody else. You get to decide how your story unfolds. Often people like to think they know our story, and they seem to think they have a say in it. They don't. It is yours and yours alone.

In Part 2, to help you navigate your own path through the forest, you will encounter a number of key fairy tale heroines who have their own story to tell. When I consider the traditional fairy tales that have been passed down through the generations, I often wonder how the protagonists in these tales would have felt about the way their stories have been told. What was their version of events? We will never know, but as we journey through the following pages, I have offered another perspective on what their life might have been like. They are all heroines in their journeys, and they have all faced their own battles in the depths of the forest. I think they can teach us a lot.

People have historically viewed these female characters as pitiful damsels in distress. They are often portrayed as naive, overly trusting, delicate females, waiting in their ornate castles to be saved by their knight in shining armour. However, the reality is many of these female protagonists have endured so much pain and heartache in their short lives. They are courageous survivors of child abuse, neglect and abandonment. In my opinion, these characters are not pathetic princesses waiting to be saved by some external force, but they are an incredible inspiration to show us that that that no matter how difficult your life has been up to this point, you can not only survive but go on to thrive. Maybe they will inspire a rising with you?

Part 2 requires you to use the journal prompts to work through the RESTORY steps. Don't overthink your answers. Just allow the truth to bubble up and show you the way. Everything you need is inside of you. You do not need to go searching for the answers. Listen to your inner child as they guide you home. Follow the thread. Listen to the whispers. Trust and believe. Go and uncover your inner light.

PART 2

NOW IT'S YOUR TURN

HOW TO USE THE RESTORY STEPS

You may find yourself going through a major life change, such as a relationship ending, illness, loss, etc. If that resonates, you can use the seven steps to help you navigate your way through this challenging time. See it as a guiding light to help you forge your own path. There is no time scale on how long this process will take. You get to decide how long you need on each step. One word of advice though: I found myself stuck in the Witch's cage for way longer than I would have liked. I found it really difficult to move from surrender to trust. This is where I started to apply the MAGIC of Movement, Alignment, Going outside, Inviting my inner child to play and Connecting. This helped me enormously in shifting out of a stage and making baby steps forwards. Find your own support system to help you move out of stagnation or indeed if you find yourself falling back a step. This isn't a linear path.

You can also use the RESTORY method on a daily basis to help you navigate your way through the general ups and downs of life. I sit down every morning and listen to what is knocking me off balance in that moment. Often it is some seemingly insignificant thing, but once again the same old patterns and limiting beliefs attempt to run the show in the background. Using the RESTORY method as a daily journaling tool helps me reprogramme these limiting thoughts and find freedom once again.

Find a notebook or journal; answer the following questions and see what comes up. Don't overthink your answers – just allow them to flow. Trust they are exactly what you need to hear. Remember the key to RESTORY-ing your life is not about throwing away who you once were but accepting all parts of you that you already are. By completing the seven steps, in order, you will learn to love and accept all parts of yourself and live your life in a truly authentic way.

Step 1

REALISE

The first stage of the RESTORY journey requires you to wake up. But wake up from what? You may have no idea that you are fast asleep. This step requires you to listen to the niggle, to listen to the whispers. Is something triggering you right now? Is someone making you angry or agitated? Do you have repeating patterns occurring in your life? Is your body trying to tell you something? These are all calls to adventure.

Remember, you have a box inside you that has stored all the unresolved pain you've shoved down over the years. Some of it you will be aware of, and some of it you won't. There are clues, but you will have to remain open to what comes up. It doesn't always make logical sense. How full is your box right now? You can answer that by considering how many distraction techniques you are relying on. The more distraction techniques, the fuller your box is.

Are you ready to wake up……?

1. What is inside your box that needs attention? What have you shoved down and are trying to distract yourself from? There may well be more than one area.

2. Select one area in your life you are least fulfilled in. (E.g. Purpose, career, relationships, health, finances etc.). When you think of this area, it will probably bring up some resistance. This is good, as it means there are still some unresolved emotions to deal with.

3. What story are you telling yourself about this aspect of your life? What is the recurring pattern, feeling, or behaviour that is showing up? Listen to the niggle. What is it trying to tell you?

The fairy tale protagonist who will guide us through this first step is Sleeping Beauty. She spent her entire childhood completely unaware she was living life under a curse. When she pricked her finger on the spinning wheel, it was only true love's kiss that could wake her. We have always been told that it was Prince Charming who woke her up, but let's consider that it was in fact her own desire to find self-love. What if she actually woke herself up?

Sleeping Beauty

Shhh.... I'm sleeping, look at my face,
So still and peaceful, not a hair out of place.
I keep my mouth shut, I'm being so good,
My voice is muted, like I promised it would.
People walk past me, without saying a word,
My stifled screams go completely unheard.
My jaw's so tender as I clamp it shut tight,
Resisting the desire to kick up a fight.
This is my destiny, according to the curse,
Held captive in this secret, unsure which is worse?
To lie dormant, patiently waiting to be saved,
Being a good girl so nicely behaved.
Or to wake myself up and face the despair,
Of this rancid secret in its revolting lair.
A restlessness causes a stirring inside,
A desire for answers can no longer hide.
The courage to wake from my amnesic sleep,
And to face the truth no matter how bleak.
For living a life that is inauthentic and fake,
Is surely no alternative to being fully awake?
As this isn't a fairy tale with a traditional plot,
With a sleeping princess acquiesced to her lot.
Waiting to be saved by some external force,
A handsome Prince on his majestic horse.
This is an invitation to journey into the unknown,
To listen to my inner child calling me home.
This is the moment I open my eyes,
And search for the truth in this web of lies.

Journal Entry

My head is throbbing as I write this. You would think being asleep for so long would leave you feeling refreshed and revitalised. Well, take it from me, it is quite the opposite. All my muscles are so tight and excruciatingly tender. I have tried to stretch to relieve the discomfort, but there is years' worth of emotions pent up in the cells of my body. It will take some time to unwind all that they have been through.

I sip the water on my bedside table to try to ease the pain in my head. I still can't quite believe what actually happened. One day I was in the top turret of the castle messing around with that old spinning wheel, then everything became a blur. I know I caught my finger on that sharp needle and watched as it ripped through the first layer of my skin. I remember seeing the droplets of red blood rise to the surface and then all went blank.

But I don't understand why that happened. People talk about a curse. Why hadn't anyone told me about it? Why was it kept a secret? This is what makes me furious. I know people were trying to protect me but how could they have kept this hidden? I keep going over it and over it in my head. Were there any signs when I was growing up? Who knew? Why were people concealing it?

I was just a child when I had my innocence taken away from me. Everyone turned a blind eye and pretended nothing was happening. Their treachery meant I was fast asleep for the best years of my life. I was stuck. I was unable to experience love, unable to allow it to permeate the core of my being.

Well, now I want answers. I woke myself up because there was something inside of me that was stronger than that curse. It was true love's kiss, but not from some random royal passer-by. It was my own desire to live my life, to discover true self-love, to find my soul's purpose. That is what woke me up.

As I think about it now, my dreams over the last few weeks had started to become more vivid. I was vaguely aware that my limbs were repeatedly twitching. There was clearly a deep niggle inside of me, urging me to open my eyes and to see the truth. Something was calling me to break through the curse, the lies, the deceit. That first gasp of air I took when I woke was like a baby's first breath when it enters this world. I guess in a way you could say this is my rebirth. I have fundamentally changed. The old me has died, and I am now filled with so much courage and desire to find answers. I have had the biggest wake-up call of all time, and I'm not going to waste it.

I have been a people-pleaser all my life. I know that is part of the role of being a Princess. People expect you to behave in a certain way, and I have been so good at it. I did exactly as my parents told me. I was being a good girl. But all the while, they were lying to me. They knew about the curse but didn't tell me. That doesn't seem right. They say they were trying to protect me but I'm not so sure. I want to find answers.

My parents are so preoccupied with what people think that they have fabricated a story about my awakening. Everyone claims I was woken up by that so-called Prince Charming riding past on his horse. They say it was true love's kiss. They are all so elated and jubilant.

They are expecting me to join in with their celebrations and dance with him in tonight's festivities as I supposedly gaze lovingly into his eyes, so eternally grateful that he saved me.

I have been telling myself I should be grateful. I am a Princess, living in a castle, with every material thing I could possibly ask for. I should feel like I am the luckiest person alive. I even have a Prince Charming waiting for me downstairs. But I don't feel any of those things. Inside I feel empty.

Everything around me is fake. There is nothing real here. No real emotions, no real conversations, no real feelings. Everyone in this Kingdom tells me what I like, they dismiss my feelings, they try to control how I feel. I am not even sure who I am anymore. I just want to be able to express how I feel, without fear of being rejected.

I am not going to pretend anymore. I will not be the grateful Princess in her beautiful ballgown. I am going to speak my truth and in doing so I am going to find my own true love.

Sleeping Beauty x

Step 2

Explore

The second stage of the RESTORY journey is stepping into the unknown and exploring all aspects of this unfamiliar land. This requires you to fully commit to going inwards and to be prepared to face this aspect of your life. Are you ready to do it?

If the answer is no, then that's ok. You cannot rush this process and you need to feel fully supported in doing this work. Remember, you do not have to do anything you do not feel ready to do. This issue is not going to go away, so you can come back to it when you feel ready.

If you are ready to dive in, then give yourself the time and space to do this work. Be kind and compassionate, but also be curious and questioning.

Are you ready to explore?

1. What emotions arise as you consider changing this aspect of your life? Are you scared, apprehensive, excited?

2. Have you tried to address this part of your life before? If so, what stopped you or held you back? Have you tried to skip around the woods and bypass going inwards? What is it about going in that you want to avoid?

3. What support systems do you have in place to help you navigate the woods?

In Step 2: Explore, we encounter a character who is very familiar with the woods: Little Red Riding Hood. Some people refer to her as an innocent and naive little girl for stopping to talk to the wolf. She is firmly told by her mother not to stray from the path and not to talk to anyone. I, however, consider her to be brave, and courageous. She was fed up with being told to fear the dangers lurking in the forest. She was ready to confront them head on. She wanted answers and to hold the wolf to account. This brought up unexpected challenges. Entering the woods requires us to move out of accepting this is just the way things are and start questioning why. This is time for us to break the old narrative and to forge a path of our own.

Little Red Riding Hood

I step outside, the air is so cold.
Hearing Mother's words 'Do as you're told.'
Nagging at me as I set off on my way,
'Stay on the path and do not stray.'
I hate being told to 'be so good.'
'To toe the line, like others would.'
The prospect of deviating fills mother with dread.
'What on earth would they say about us, Red?'
I don't give a damn what the others would say.
Just watch, I'm going to forge my own way.
I close the door and step out into the wood,
I pull on my cloak and lift up my hood.
Every footstep of mine pounding the earth,
Leading me closer to my self–worth.
Curiosity guides me, leading the way,
Venturing deeper as I begin to stray.
Clambering over trees fallen to the ground,
Unsure where I'm going, there's an unfamiliar sound.
A rustling overhead in the canopy of trees,
The crack of a branch, I immediately freeze.
My senses are heightened, my eyes open wide,
What's lurking in the shadows, where can I hide?
Then I pause and remember why I am here,
Courage urging me on, in spite of the fear.
I have one simple mission, one truth to uncover,
As I continue on my path towards my Grandmother.

I am here to disclose the deceit and the lies,
Of the revolting wolf and his sickening disguise.
Skulking around as if he's so honourable and kind,
Fooling others with his act, they're totally blind.
If he didn't want me to speak in such a way,
He should've behaved better, not used me as prey.
No one will silence me as I stand my ground.
I have too much to gain, forever unbound.
Let's put on our cloaks, and pull up our hoods,
We have a path to uncover as we go into the woods.

Journal Entry

Today as I walked through the forest, I had to pause and lean against the trunk of the giant old Oak tree to calm my breathing. I inhaled deeply and exhaled slowly, just as the therapist taught me. I tried to release the knot of tension that had worked its way up into my chest. My heart was pounding. No matter how many times I travel through that forest, when the light fades, it always gets me. The unfamiliar sounds all seem so much louder as the sun sets. I am jumpy, on edge, anticipating the worst.

It's been over a year now. I thought the fear would have gone but I think it will always be with me. My body forever holding a trace of the events of that day. Even though I know he is locked away and unable to get me, I still fear his breath on the back of my neck. His stench filling my nostrils. I feel the nausea threatening to rise. That filthy, loathsome wolf.

The wind started to build so I pulled my cloak a little tighter around my body. I'm really thankful for the fur lining Grandmother had sewn in. I pulled up my hood. The thick red fabric blocking out the intensity of the cold air. I'd forgotten how harsh the winters were. The chill went right through to my bones. I'm still feeling it now, even though I've been sitting in front of the fire, as I write this.

My mind travels back to that fateful day. I don't regret straying from the path. I know people said, 'I told you so,' and 'You should have been a good girl and stayed on the path,' but why should I? Why should I be intimidated by the parasites who skulk around these parts in their elaborate disguises? I can see through their sickening deceit, and I am not afraid to call them out. Everyone else seems to be so keen to turn a blind eye and pretend it isn't happening. Well, I'm not. I am going to speak my truth.

There is so much fear around the forest. Yes, there are wolves in disguise. Yes, they will trick you. But we must stand up to them. Too often we are afraid to step into the unknown for the fear of what we might uncover. Together we must find the courage to rise up against these despicable creatures. We will not be made to feel like we are bad in any way. They are the bad ones. We must take a stand.

Little Red
Riding Hood

Step 3

see the
shadows

The third stage of the RESTORY journey is See the Shadows. Here we encounter the Wicked Witch. There is no getting round this phase. The Wicked Witch will speak in absolute terms. She will use words such as 'never', 'should', and 'always'. My Wicked Witch would tell me, '*You are totally unworthy of love. Who in their right mind would love you if they really knew what you really were? You have always been vile, revolting and filthy. You should be ashamed of yourself. You deserve to rot in hell.*'

Facing our shadows is the only way to heal. The Wicked Witch can actually be our greatest teacher. Remember she is a wise old woman, who can appear either as a friend or a foe depending on your sense of worth.

Surrender to your shadow side

1. What is the Wicked Witch saying about this aspect of you and your life? Let her vent it all out, no holding back. What is really lurking down there?

   Draw a picture, write a poem, write a song, allow this side of you to be fully expressed. What does it look like, and feel like?

2. Allow yourself to be with these emotions. Release the emotions, feel the emotions. Watch to see if you try to run away from them. Try not to run away: face them and allow them to teach you your truth.

3. Breathe and surrender. Listen to a meditation or practice some breathing techniques to allow these emotions to be released.

Step 3: See the Shadows, introduces us to Gretal. She has endured so much heartache. Her parents took her to the woods and left her and her brother to die. She was then captured by the Wicked Witch. Gretal shows us that no matter what trauma she has encountered in her young life, she is able to confront her shadows and surrender to their wisdom. This ultimately sets her free.

Gretal

Another night kept in this Gingerbread hell,
With its sugar–coated walls and sickly smell.
Tormenting me as the Witch loudly snores,
My muscles aching from the endless chores.
I gaze through the bars of this desolate cage,
And feel anger erupting, overflowing with rage.
I was abandoned in the woods, left to die,
I'm searching for the answers, keep asking why?
Is it because I am bad inside?
I thought I was good, I really tried.
It's all my fault, I'm totally to blame,
It's dragging me under, the waves of shame.
These shadows are looming, creeping towards me,
I'm stuck in this prison, nowhere to flee.
The only option I have is to let go of control,
To surrender, allow them to swallow me whole.
As the anger and the guilt permeate my being,
Unravelling the emotions, I've been afraid of seeing.
Exposing the fear of my unlovable side,
My worthlessness has nowhere to hide.
It's here as I lie on the cold, damp floor,
These shadows in me, can hurt me no more.
I accept them, welcome their existence with grace,
They are part of me, their pain leaves a trace.
They are breadcrumbs leading me with compassion,
Towards my true self, my purpose, my passion.
As I fully integrate all aspects of me,
I'm no longer locked up, I'm totally free.

As I leave my confinement and open the door
Killing the Witch, she can hurt me no more
I am not a bad person, it wasn't my fault
I was the target of a heinous assault
I have opened myself up to an expansive space,
I wipe away the tears that have stained my face.
I learned to surrender, and it set me free.
It's time to step boldly into the next chapter of me.

Journal Entry

You would have thought living in a Gingerbread House with cakes and sweets adorning every wall and window frame would have been heavenly. It was, the very first day my brother and I stumbled across it. We were starving. We'd only eaten berries for days on end so that first taste of the sweetly spiced bread was utter heaven. I remember eating so much that my belly ached.

Then the harsh reality hit home. Not only had we been abandoned in the woods and left to die by our own family, but the little old lady who offered us shelter was in fact a carnivorous Witch. In a way I was grateful that she used me to do all the chores as it gave me something to do during the day, enabling me to stifle out the agonising voice inside my own head. I had started to believe the Witch's vile words that I was a bad person, rotten to the core. Once those toxic thoughts enter your head, it's really hard to silence them. The only way I found to minimise their impact was to keep myself extremely busy, sweeping the biscuit floors, polishing the windows with sugar syrup and patching up the cake roof. That was one job that required a lot of effort as the forest birds loved to feast on the cake roof. The smell was overpowering. I used to love sweets and cakes, but I honestly do not think I will ever eat anything made from refined sugar ever again!

At night, I had no choice but to lie on the floor of the cage and allow the hateful words to wash over me. One after another, in the darkness, they poked and prodded at my sense of self. I have no idea how long I had been trapped by their vile assault. I tried to fight them, hide from them, control them. I tried to drown them out by focusing on the Witch's guttural snores.

Then one day, exhausted and defeated, I stopped fighting, and something incredible happened. It's really hard to explain but it was as if the noxious emotions started to lose their potency. Once I surrendered to them and let them out of me, they were no longer inside of me, eating me up. Actually feeling them was not as terrifying as the thought of feeling them. I allowed each one to spill out of me and then once they were out, they shrivelled up and skulked away. Each time I released one, there was less and less anguish inside of me. They created space inside of me and in that space I found the courage to get out of that hell hole.

I had somehow allowed myself to believe that I deserved to be locked up in a vile house being tortured by a malevolent carnivore, that I had brought it on myself, that I was to blame. As I voiced these emotions and allowed them to pour out of me, I was able to see how absurd they were.

I was an innocent child, I was not bad. I had been abandoned by my family and captured by a Wicked Witch, but I wasn't bad. I was, in fact, immensely brave. I had endured so much and yet I was still alive.

I had been scared of the emotions bubbling up inside of me but I had to break the pattern of ignoring them. They were trying to get my attention. As soon as gave them the attention they craved, as soon as I surrendered to them, I realised I was in fact free.

Gretal

Step 4

trust

The fourth stage of the RESTORY journey is Trust. This is where we let go of the logical mind that is trying to offer you rational thought. Trust requires you to take a leap even if you have no idea where you are going to land.

This is the stage of the journey where you will go inwards and meet your inner child. Trust that they know the way home. Trust that they will show you the path to light you up and lead you to the future that you have been dreaming of.

Trust what your inner child has to say.

1. What is your inner child trying to tell you? Where has this limiting belief come from? Ask them and listen. Sit quietly with your eyes closed and listen to the whispers. Can you feel the tug?

2. Allow your inner child to write. Pick up the pen and write. Don't think about it: just see what comes up.

3. Where in your body do you feel it? Trust your body. It is telling you what emotions are locked up, waiting to be released.

Step 4: Trust, takes us to meet Cinderella. In the traditional tale, our protagonist waited to be saved by her Fairy Godmother. However, this version of the tale does not see Cinderella waiting for her Fairy Godmother to grant her wishes, but rather sees her trusting herself that she can make her own dreams come true. She believed in magic and knew deep down that she deserved to have a better future, one that was more in alignment with her core values.

Cinderella

Why do they hate me? What have I done?
These vile stepsisters and their spiteful mum.
Constantly bullying with their insults and threats,
No sign of remorse, no hint of regret.
I've put up with enough, I'm taking no more.
No servant life for me, not a single chore.
I deserve to be treated with dignity and respect,
No more abuse, no more neglect.
I will not sit around feeling sorry for my life,
With all of its stress and the constant strife.
I'll break these shackles that have held me so tight,
Manifest a life that's beautiful and bright.
I don't need a fairy with a magic wand,
To transport me to a life beyond.
I don't need a pumpkin nor a beautiful dress,
There is no Prince Charming I'm trying to impress.
Glass slippers are pointless, they fall off and break,
I cannot risk anything, there's too much at stake.
There is a life out there waiting to be found,
I'm not going to miss it by hanging around.
I trust myself fully, I have too much to gain,
There's a much better existence calling my name.
I pull off my rags and throw down my broom,
I push open the door from this stifling room.
I am worthy of a life filled with joy and laughter,
That goes past midnight, into my happily ever after.
I finally leave this miserable existence behind
And head to a future that's beautifully aligned.

Journal Entry

When I think back to that time in my life, I can hardly believe it actually happened. I have come on so much since those dark days. The therapy has really helped me to resolve the years of abuse I received at the hands of my stepmother and stepsisters. They were vile. I am so glad I finally stood up for myself and reported them. They deserve everything they got.

The worst part of it all was I believed their taunts and lies. It started off slowly to begin with, a snide comment here, a lie there. It's like they were turning up the heat so slowly that I didn't realise how much damage it was doing until I was in so much pain. It made me question myself, doubt my own memories and perceptions. Some dark nights I really did question my own sanity. It gradually undermined my confidence to the point where I was unable to fully distinguish what was the truth and what was false.

I was so grateful for that invitation that came through the door to the Royal Ball. When they told me I couldn't go because I wasn't worthy, part of me shrivelled up and accepted their truth. Why would a filthy, pathetic person like me be accepted at such an opulent party? But it also planted a seed. Seeing the gold lettering on the thick, luxurious cream card activated something inside of me. I felt the tug in my core, a deep urge to break free from this miserable existence and live the life I was destined to live.

Gradually I started to trust myself, trust the niggle that was inside of me, trying to remind me of my truth, my future. One that was filled with love, happiness, joy, creativity, colour, light. Not this dark, depressing, monotonous existence that revolved around chores and responsibility.

It stirred something deep within me. My body responded and the more I leaned into that, the less I tried to rationalise it with logic. I know this was something that required a leap of faith. This wasn't a well—thought—out, practical plan. This was one giant leap of faith into the unknown. Just like the acorn holds an entire oak tree within its tiny shell, I too felt like I was a great expanse of wonder constricted in a body wrapped in rags and self—doubt. It was time to break free. I deserved more.

I jumped and trusted that I would be held. I had no idea where I was going to land, but I knew that there was a future for me that was way beyond this reality. Sometimes you have to just go for it and trust that the Universe will catch you.

Cinderella

Step 5

orientate

The fifth stage of the RESTORY journey is Orientate. This step requires us to become really clear on what we want in life. Clarity is key here. Is it what you really want or what you think you ought to do? This step is all about removing the mask and being fully honest about what you want, and what boundaries you want to put in place.

What do YOU really want?

1. What are your values? List between three to five core values that are important to you.

2. Think about Future-You. What lights you up? What boundaries do you have in place? How is your life different to your life today?

3. Check in with your inner child. What do they want? Check it is what they really want and not what they think they ought to do.

The character who will support us through this step is Goldilocks. She is not afraid to say what she wants. In this version we learn that Goldilocks has been living her life trying to please others and has not followed her heart. As she stands in the bears' cottage in the middle of the woods, for the first time she feels courageous enough to go after what she wants, no longer settling for what she thinks she ought to do.

Goldilocks

I've been running for hours, I'm completely lost,
The ground is hard, covered in frost.
I spot a cottage with a warm inviting glow,
I take small tentative footsteps, going so slow.
I knock on the door, but nobody replies,
It is slightly ajar, which comes as a surprise.
The aroma of sweet porridge hangs in the air,
The owners of the house can't be seen anywhere.
I haven't eaten for days, my stomach loudly groans,
My body is exhausted, I ache through to my bones.
I step into the house and wait for someone to come,
Warming my feet which have become numb.
I am ravenous and stare at the porridge in the bowl,
I hear the message coming from the core of my soul.
Go after your dreams, don't wait to be saved,
You've spent too many years being enslaved.
Follow your desires, live your life in alignment,
No more settling for a life locked in confinement.
Seek out your dreams, step up and be brave,
Follow your heart, and do what it craves.
For the first time in my life I feel daring and bold,
I taste the first bowl, but the porridge is cold.
I move onto the next which burns my tongue,
Then the third, clearly for someone quite young.
The bowl is so small, but it tastes divine,
I eat the whole lot, as if it were mine.

I accidentally break one of the chairs,
I need to lie down, so I climb up the stairs.
I'm exhausted from running for days on end,
I need to rest, I can no longer pretend.
I lie on the bed and feel myself weep,
My eyes gently close, I fall fast asleep.
Healing is painful, it cannot be rushed,
It takes time for the body to adapt and adjust.
This is not a time to be harsh and judgmental,
But tender, compassionate, loving and gentle.

Journal Entry

For as long as I can remember I have been trying to please everyone else, pushing my own needs to one side. I'm not sure when it happened, but over time I just seemed to lose touch with what I wanted or felt. It was safer to do what other people wanted. Pleasing others meant I was being a good girl.

I would always feel really exhausted and struggled to let people down when inside I was screaming 'Just say no!' I seemed completely unable to put myself first. I was terrified of what people would think of me. I felt that if I was a good girl and helped everyone else, then nobody would see the real me, the bad girl that was hiding inside. The problem was, all this people-pleasing and ignoring my own feelings left me exhausted and resentful.

Then one day, it all got too much and I exploded. I ran into the woods and kept running until I found that quaint little cottage. I was broken and desperately needed to rest. I had always found it so difficult to ask for help but that day I was ready to accept any help I could get. I could no longer live my life trying to please others and then feeling dreadful if someone disliked me. No matter how many people I tried to please, I would never feel happy or fulfilled. The only person who could make me feel happy and fulfilled was me.

I was so grateful to discover that cottage with the delicious porridge on the table. Normally, I would have gone looking for the owners, to tell them they had left the door open. Or I would have waited patiently outside in the cold, but that was the old me. I had made a promise to myself that I would no longer put other people's needs before my own. I was exhausted, absolutely starving and so cold. I decided I was going to go into the cottage and warm myself up.

When I smelled the delicious aroma of porridge in the air, I just knew I had to eat it. I was famished. The first bowl was cold. The old me, would have just eaten it and ensured the cottage owners had the warm porridge. But not that day. That day I made sure I was going to get the best meal and eat the porridge that was 'just right'.

As I was devouring the porridge, I accidentally broke the little chair. I promised I would repair it just after I had a little lie down. I was so tired. I tried all the beds and found one that was so comfortable. I curled up on the bed and let the tears flow. I felt so warm and safe. It was the first time in a long time I had allowed myself to let go and feel the emotions deep inside of me. I must have eventually nodded off.

I have no idea how long I was asleep, but when I woke up there were three not very happy bears staring at me. In the past, I would have immediately leapt up and started to apologise profusely, fearful that would dislike me and think I was rude. But something had shifted in me. I was no longer going to be a perpetual people-pleaser. Instead, I stayed in the comfy bed and sobbed. I explained what events had lead me to their door. And the amazing thing was they didn't hate me. They made me a cup of tea and fetched a warm blanket. They were so kind. They invited me to stay for dinner. I really wanted to stay there in the warmth, so I did. I listened to what my heart wanted and responded from a place of self-compassion and self-love. It felt really empowering to honour my own needs.

Mummy Bear was such a nurturing, loving bear and I opened myself up to receive her nourishment. I stayed with the bears for a couple of weeks until I was feeling strong again. I ate delicious soup and slept so much. Baby Bear was really kind and let me have his bed and he slept in his mum's bed. I worked out who I was and what I wanted in my life. I became really clear on what my values were and made sure I didn't allow myself to get swept away with what others wanted. I left that cottage with clear boundaries, and it felt so good.

Goldilocks

Step 6

reclaim
your power

The sixth stage of the RESTORY journey is Reclaim Your Power. This is where you piece yourself back together again. Remember this is like the Japanese art of kintsugi, where you piece back together any broken pieces of pottery with gold, making the finished product more beautiful and stronger than before. By embracing our imperfections and flaws and actually highlighting our scars, we can rise up stronger and more resilient than before.

All of you is welcome.

1. List your key strengths in this area of your life. What is already going well for you?

2. List any fears in this area. Allow any past mistakes to surface and accept them all without judgement.

3. Forgive yourself and offer yourself kindness and compassion. Remind your inner child that they are ok.

Here on the sixth step of the journey: Reclaim Your Power, we encounter Snow White. She is learning to accept all parts of herself. She finds freedom in her honesty. She doesn't have to pretend with the dwarves. She doesn't need that brave face. She can let her true emotions out. They love and accept her exactly as she is. Even though her evil stepmother tries numerous attempts to kill her, she rises, stronger than before. She gathers together all the parts of herself that she abandoned on the way. She embraces the fear, shame, guilt, and regret. She welcomes these parts of her in. By doing so, she reclaims her power once more.

Snow White

Lately I've focused on nourishment and rest
Taking time to replenish, I feel truly blessed.
Even when evil comes knocking at my door,
I refuse to get embroiled in that anymore.
This time has taught me to be honest and wild,
To play and create with my inner child.
To accept all parts of me previously hidden,
Saying 'I'm fine' is now completely forbidden.
The dwarves have accepted all parts of me,
Whether grumpy, or bashful, dopey or sleepy.
There is no part of me I dread to face,
I accept all parts of me, in a warm embrace.
I am whole, I am complete, I'm not afraid to say,
There are many sides to me and that is ok.
Now when I look in the mirror on the wall,
I accept that I am fair after all.
A poison apple will not trick me into believing,
That I am unworthy, no more deceiving.
I'm no longer scared of being captured and killed,
For I'm following my heart, I'm being fulfilled.
This tale will end with me confronting my fears,
No longer hiding, suppressing silent tears.
I allow all of me to shine without shame,
This is my life, not a stupid game.
My free will is such a formidable gift,
As I reclaim my power, the energy shifts.
Snow White is my name and watch as I rise,
With strength in my bones and hope in my eyes.

Journal Entry

I cannot begin to tell you how different I feel after spending time in that delightful cottage with those incredible dwarves. They taught me the importance of self-care. I used to feel so guilty for taking time out to look after myself, but they taught me that treating myself with kindness and compassion was like taking essential vitamins and minerals. It was as important as eating or sleeping. It took quite some practice though. At first, I didn't think I deserved it. I felt guilty for all the bad thoughts I had about my stepmother. I felt bad about hating that stupid mirror. I also felt ashamed that I actually enjoyed hearing the words that I was the fairest of them all. I must be so conceited. That fuelled my inner critic who relished telling me I was a spoilt brat and deserved to die.

I have kept these feelings inside of me for so long. It was exhausting carrying them around with me all the time, whilst pretending I was happy and fine. It was hard work being such a good girl for the whole palace to witness. That winter's evening when the dwarves encouraged me to share these hidden parts of me was the most terrifying and comforting at the same time.

When I started to tell them about these sides to me, I was so fearful that they would throw me out of their house, and I would get eaten by wild animals.

But they didn't. It was the most peculiar thing. As I shared yet another shameful side to myself, I just felt lighter and lighter. They didn't judge me or rebuke me. In fact, they said it made them love me even more, for it showed my vulnerability.

Doc explained that we all have these hidden parts to ourselves, and by allowing them all to be present and loving and accepting each and every one, we were able to fully love ourselves. It was made even easier when they invited my inner child out to play. I had forgotten about her. She disappeared just after my mother died and my dad remarried that horrid woman. That's when I was told to grow up and be a good girl. I lost touch with my playful side. But the dwarves, particularly Happy and Dopey have helped me to reclaim that part of me that I thought was lost.

We have had so much fun, dancing, singing, writing stories and creating shadow puppets with our hands. Dopey does a brilliant three-legged horse! He's still working on the fourth leg. So now, even when the fear comes tapping on the windowpane, I have nothing to run away from, there is nothing to hide. No part of me is weak or embarrassing. There are no secrets hiding inside of me and this feels so liberating. I am so excited to begin this next chapter of my life.

Snow White

Step 7

you
decide

The final stage of the RESTORY journey is You Decide. Remember, the RESTORY method is not about throwing away who you are and totally reinventing yourself. It is about accepting all parts of yourself and making small steps towards Future-You.

You will come up against the old looping patterns that you have faced time and time again. That's ok. Go gently with yourself. This isn't a magic pill that will change things over night. It is all about taking small steps in the right direction. Support yourself with kind words of encouragement.

Ultimately, you are the only person who can do it. This is your story, and you get to decide how it unfolds. You need to be consciously aware that you want to change this aspect of your life, and then you can start to build a small habit that will lead you there.

Don't wait for the Fairy Godmother to wave her magic wand and do the work for you. It's up to you.

Are you ready to create change?

1. Set your intention: Become really clear on what aspect of your life you wish to change.

2. Make a change: Commit to one small step to support you in this process.

3. Support yourself: Write a positive affirmation to support you.

The final character we encounter in this journey is the Fairy Godmother. She is a sage woman who has witnessed many dreams coming true. She does, however, have some wise words on manifesting your future-self and what some of the main pitfalls are. Let her guide you on the final stages of your journey: You decide.

Fairy Godmother

I hear your wishes as you kneel down and pray
That all your dreams will be answered one day
Your manifestations are received loud and clear
As you wait for them all to magically appear.

These fairy tale stories have a lot to answer for
Giving people hope there'll be a knock on the door
A wave of a wand all your dreams magically appear
A puff of smoke and everything comes clear

A bigger house here, a new relationship there
Money in the bank and long luscious hair
A life filled with purpose, that lights up the heart
A brand—new car, and a fancy piece of art

You can manifest it all, with your focused attention
Releasing all your fears and any pent—up tension
But you cannot just sit and wait for it to come
It requires focus and the work to be done

So, by all means wish, and dream and pray
Manifest the life you want to live your way
But to make magic happen, that comes down to you
You're the only one to make your wishes come true.

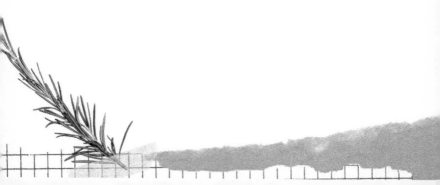

Journal Entry

I am so happy when I discover someone who is willing to the work. There seems to be this myth that you just have to think positive thoughts and they will just happen. It's driving me mad when I see people wasting their lives sitting and waiting and sitting and waiting. You cannot just think positively and then everything will magically appear. I wish it were that simple. The problem with this approach is I see so many people feeling disappointed that they are unable to manifest their dreams.

Of course, I believe in magic. How can a Fairy Godmother not believe in magic? Magic is all around us. The Universe is continually sending us opportunities and gifts, but we have to do the work to receive them. The people that I have seen achieve the most manifestation success are those who have reprogrammed their self–limiting beliefs. They have ventured inwards and looked at all their shadows and started unpeeling the layers.

There will always be layers. We are never finished. There are always opportunities for us to grow and evolve. Even us Fairy Godmothers! But if we are committed to doing the work, then we will start to live the life we desire.

It all starts with an intention, a clear focus of what we want and then we must take action to enable progress to happen. This can just be small steps, every day. It doesn't have to be a dramatic overhaul. So many people think the current version of themselves is no good, and they try to throw the whole lot away and replace it with a shinier, sparklier version. This is never advisable.

The key for me is loving and accepting who you already are, even the uncomfortable bits. Going into the forest to make friends with the shadows is what makes the difference. Everything you need to become future–you is already inside you. The gemstone has been there all along. You just didn't realise. You do not need to look for it externally. It is not outside of you. Follow the thread home and go make that magic happen!

Fairy
Godmother ☆

Share Your Restory Journey

"There is no greater agony than bearing an untold story inside you." – Maya Angelou

Storytelling has always offered a deeply powerful path to healing. It unites people, encourages empathy, and takes us to places we may never have dared to explore. When we hear stories told from the hearts of others, it stirs something deep within us. It ignites a fire that encourages us to boldly forge our own way. The brave, courageous female fairy tale protagonists shared their own unique stories with us. They have shown us that despite the neglect, abuse, abandonment, death threats, incarceration and assault they have each encountered, they have been able to rise. They have shown us it is possible to rewrite the narrative. They took control of their destiny and they decided how their story unfolds.

I hope as you have journeyed through this book, you have been inspired to take ownership of your own story and forge your own path through the woods. The woods are transformative and if you are prepared to step into the unknown, they will uncover your own 'happily ever after'.

Personally, I have been completely transformed by this incredible process. The gemstone within me shines a light so vibrantly that it calls out to other brave women who are ready to embark on their own journey. I fully believe that every time one of us finds the courage to speak up, we inspire others to do the same. Speaking our truth requires great strength, but it is unbelievably liberating and empowering.

Share your true authentic voice. Tell your story. Rewrite your narrative. When you do, it will inspire others and together we will rise.

The Rising

Sisters, I feel you, I hear you, I'm with you

From the ashes of the fire.
We begin to rise.
Hope and determination,
Reflected in our eyes.
The tears of our pain,
Have left their trace.
As they fell from our souls,
And stained our face.
Rising together,
We stood our ground.
Permitting our secrets,
To finally be found.
Gathering together,
Sisters we heal.
Expressing the truth,
Of every emotion we feel.
No more muting our voices,
To hide the pain.
Our suffering will not,
Be held in vain.
We threw away the masks,
That shielded our grief.
We peeled away layers,
We're raw underneath.

No more pretending,
Being kept in a cage.
Let's vent our emotions,
Our anger and rage.
We were never broken,
Nor rotten to the core.
You cannot abuse us,
Anymore.
We are brave, courageous,
Sisters who stand.
Reclaiming our power,
Of this sacred land.
Held by the everlasting,
Pulse of the Earth.
This is our revival,
Our expansive rebirth.
Gathering together,
We unite as one.
Sisters, Rise!
There's work to be done.
We are the heroes,
In the narrative of life.
Brave and courageous,
We wield the knife.
Severing generational trauma,
Ending it now.
Breaking the promises,
The silent vow.

Gathering together,
We unite as one.
Sisters, rise,
Our story's just begun.
Assessing the state,
Of the war–torn terrain.
We know in our hearts,
Life will never be the same.
As we look in the mirror,
We love what we see.
There's no sense of dread,
Nor a need to flee.
We've faced every fragment,
Of our shattered soul.
We are complete,
We finally feel whole.
The shame, the grief,
The anger, the regret.
They are all part of us,
No need to forget.
We soothed away the ache,
Of discomfort in our core.
When we picked ourselves up,
From the forest floor.
The child within each of us,
Is safe and sound.
No longer disconnected,
They have all been found.

Sisters, it's time,
Follow the thread back home.
Guided by the light,
From the precious gemstone.
Let's RESTORY our lives,
In every chapter we write.
Caressing our scars,
In our courageous fight.

Sisters, I feel you,
Sisters, I hear you,
Sisters, I'm with you.

ACKNOWLEDGEMENTS

Thank you to my amazing husband, Richard, for being my constant rock, and my two wonderful children Millie & Ollie. I couldn't have written this book without your unwavering support. I love you all so much.

Thank you also to my two spaniels Willow & Woody who were by my side, every step of this journey. Your snuggles were my medicine.

Finally thank you "Little Katie' for not giving up hope, for having the courage to tell your story and for guiding me back home. I love you.

About the Author

Katie Jones is a writer, certified Yoga teacher, Reiki practitioner, and wellbeing coach. Katie is passionate about delving into the magic of inner child healing, chakra balancing, narrative therapy and positive psychology. Her body tingles when she is encircled by enchanted trees and connected to elemental energies.

Connect with Katie:
Website: www.andthenkatie.com
Instagram: @andthenkatie

Lightning Source UK Ltd.
Milton Keynes UK
UKHW010634260521
384407UK00001B/131